C000221696

The Hours

of

Our Lady

The Little Office of the Blessed Virgin Mary

and
the Office for the Dead

Table of Contents

Introduction

The Hours of Our Lady is based on the 1867 edition of the Little Office of the Blessed Virgin Mary published 1869 in Dublin by John Fowler and compared with the 1915 Benziger edition. Some modifications in layout were undertaken to aid in clarity, with rubrics included in the text, to make it easier for those who wish to make these prayers their own to do so easily, and according to the mind of the Church.

Those of us devoted to Our Lady will appreciate that this short prayer allows them not only to sanctify the day with prayer, alone or with others, but to do so using a text, hymns, and anthems that are simple and reverent. Its elevated language exemplifies noble simplicity and unembellished piety, in the most beautiful tradition of good liturgical prayer. The prayers and hymns as well are of high quality and much used translation, and are a pleasure to read and sing.

And the hymns and anthems should be sung! The depth of Catholic hymnody throughout history is due more to her liturgical life outside of Mass than it is within the Mass, and the Breviary and other Offices have always been sung by the Church. This English only translation takes this challenge seriously, and you will find within these pages suggestions for appropriate and well known hymn tunes at the heading of each hymn.

My hope is that Our Lady will be pleased to hear again this particular form of the Little Office on the lips of her children. My prayer is that it might bring you closer to her divine Son, and fortify you for daily apostolate.

Jim Garlits

These praises and prayers
I lay at thy feet,
O Virgin of virgins,
O Mary most sweet.

Be Thou my true guide
Through this pilgrimage here,
And stand by my side
When death draweth near.

The Hours of Our Lady

The Office of the B.V.M.

Based on the Introductions to the Office of the Blessed Virgin Mary and the Office of the Dead by Fowler (1869) and Benziger (1915), with emendations by the editor.

The Little Office of the Blessed Virgin Mary is of ancient usage in the Church, and was recited by the clergy and devout laity, and practiced by rule in religious monasteries, even from the seventh century.

This Office was instituted by the Church, guided by the Spirit of God, with a shorter format than the Breviary, and is divided into seven canonical hours, according to the following order:

- Vespers
- Compline
- Matins with Lauds
- Prime
- Terce
- Sext
- None

The Little Office of the Blessed Virgin Mary is always of a simple rite, and as such, it should be recited every day, and invariably observed the whole year round. The simple rite signifies that the office commences at Vespers, and terminates at None, that there be said only one nocturn at Matins. The psalms are changed according to the order of the days, with the First Nocturn recited on Sunday, Monday, and Thursday. The Second Nocturn is recited on Tuesday and Friday. The Third Nocturn is recited on Wednesday and Saturday.

This version of the Office retains the Commemoration of the Saints after the prayers in Vespers and Lauds; however the Anthems of the Psalms are said in their entirety before and after, as in the edition made possible by the changes after Pope Benedict XVI issued *Summorum Pontificum*. The Anthems, Prayers, and Lessons of this Little Office change at different times in the year, as in Advent, at Christmas time, in Paschal time, and the rest of the year. These changes are marked in the Office by the time of the year as may be observed by the reader.

As noted in the in text rubrics:

- The Office in Advent begins at Vespers on Saturday before the first Sunday of Advent, until None on Christmas Eve.
- The Office at Christmas begins at Vespers on the vigil of Christmas, continuing until Vespers on the second of February, which is the feast of the Purification.
- The common Office begins at Matins on the second of February, continuing until None on Saturday before the first Sunday in Advent.
- Paschal time is from Vespers on Easter Saturday, continuing until None on Saturday the week after Pentecost.

The hymn *Te Deum* is a devotional practice introduced in the Office, and it may be said after the third lesson of the Nocturn all times of the year, except during Advent, and from the ninth Sunday before Easter (Septuagesima Sunday) until Easter. It may be likewise said on the feasts of the Blessed Virgin Mary in Advent and Lent, that is, on the 8th and 18th of December, on the 25th of March, and on the second of February, if it comes after Septuagesima Sunday.

Note: When these days fall on Sunday, the *Te Deum* is said in the Sunday office and not on the following Monday, although the feast of the Blessed Virgin Mary may be transferred to Monday in the Divine Office on account of the privilege of Sunday. Second, as the Matins for the day are usually said in the preceding evening, this hymn is then added to the office.

Speaking on the time of day at which the different hours should be prayed:

- Vespers and Compline were traditionally prayed by monastics in the late afternoon, however, it is more common now for the laity to pray Vespers in the late afternoon and Compline right before retiring to bed.
- Matins with Lauds can be prayed during the night, being nocturns, but again this can present difficulties for the laity, and can be prayed instead early in the morning before sunrise.
- Prime is prayed at 6 a.m.
- Terce is prayed at 9 a.m.
- Sext is prayed at noon
- None is prayed at 3 p.m., ending the liturgical day.

The names of Biblical books and the numbering of the Psalms has been adapted to the modern usage to make it easier for the modern reader to navigate.

As noted earlier, this edition of the Office is equally suited for individual recitation, as well as by groups of the faithful where possible. The verses are set up so as to be taken in turns by two individuals or groups. Rubrics are in gray, with passages normally kept short to hold the reader's attention, are set apart by asterisks * and where the verses are divided between two individuals or "choirs;" and red crosses + indicate where one is to make the Sign of the Cross. At the name of Jesus, one should bow profoundly. At the name of Mary, one should bow the head and shoulders. At the name of a Saint, one should bow the head.

Some common terms used when praying the Office with others are Presider, Cantor, Choir, and Reader. The Presider has certain roles, as shown in the rubrics interspersed with the text. The Cantor leads a Choir, and will say the Anthem and then the first half line of the Psalm, then the opposite Choir will continue that line. Note that this entails that there are two Choirs. At the end of a Psalm, the Cantor will again recite the Anthem, then the other Cantor will stand and begin the next Anthem, and so on. Cantors also start the Versicles, and the Choirs respond together. The Choirs consist of all those praying under their Cantors, and they will alternate their lines with the opposite Choir.

When three or more people are praying the Office in common, all the roles should be assigned. When three are praying in common, obviously the two Cantors will also assume the roles of their Choir. If only two are praying in common, one of the two Cantors should also assume the role of the Presider, and Readers should be assigned however is sensible, perhaps the person not acting as Presider. The Readers historically recited their readings in order of "dignity," which speaks of the dignity of office, not personal dignity, but since the laity hold no such offices, the readings can be recited by one person, alternate between two people, or be assigned with larger groups. When one person is praying the Office alone, obviously he or she assumes all of the roles. It is entirely possible to learn the music and ceremonial of this Office in a week, since the hymns and anthems are simple, and extensive rubrics are interspersed with the text.

From the 1915 Benziger introduction, the author suggests that under all circumstances, when praying the Office of Our Lady, we must place our hand in hers, and together with her, approach the

Throne of Grace. St. Augustine says, "Let it not be objected that the words of the Office are not our own, that the Psalms were not composed for us, that they suppose thoughts, circumstances, and dispositions that are not ours. The Psalms have Jesus as their principal object. They express the mind of all Christians considered in Him who is their divine head. The feelings contained in the Psalms are those which were felt first in the soul of Our Lord by the Holy Ghost, and then through Him in all those who are members of His mystical body. They are as much ours as David's, or any of the Saints."

The Little Office is a choral service, that is, deriving of a public service either sung or recited with a certain ceremonial. The importance of posture, gesture, and attitude in liturgical prayer cannot be overstated, even when prayed in private or alone. St Paul tells us "Let all things be done decently and according to order." Keep in mind that the Church decks her public prayer with a minute code of rules and ceremonies, not as a burden but as a joy which is inspired by the spirit of reverence. When we pray the Little Office, we should strive to honor the ceremonials she has ordained, since it has been calculated to help our souls retain or regain the presence of God.

At the time of this printing, this book is provided for private devotion, which can include families and groups, understanding that in some places the Little Office is still prayed as a liturgical office. Since the Council more emphasis has been placed on praying the Liturgy of the Hours, but there are some religious orders that still observe these Hours. For the laity and for active contemplatives, praying the Liturgy of the Hours can be time consuming and expensive.

As presented here, these hours are for no third orders, tertiaries, or oblates. I present it for the private recitation of those who have been enrolled in and invested with the Brown Scapular of Our Lady of Mount Carmel. In that sense, we are members of Carmel by Confraternity, as Our Lady wished when she gave the Scapular to St. Simon Stock. There is much within these pages that is worthy of meditation. Pray it, sing it, and let it sink into the deepest recesses of your being.

Before & After Prayers

Kneel

Before the Office

Open thou, O Lord, my mouth to bless thy holy name. Cleanse my heart from all vain, perverse, and distracting thoughts, enlighten my understanding, inflame my will, that I may worthily perform this Little Office and may deserve to be heard in the presence of thy divine Majesty, through Christ our Lord, Amen.

I offer up to thee these hours, and unite my intention with that of Jesus Christ, thy Son, who, while on earth, rendered you the most acceptable homage of divine praises.

Hail Mary, full of grace, the Lord is with thee. Blessed art thou among women and blessed is the fruit of thy womb, Jesus. Holy Mary, Mother of God, pray for us sinners, now and in the hour of our death. Amen.

After the Office

(Presider) Everlasting praise, honor, power, and glory be given by all creatures to the most holy and undivided Trinity, to the Humanity of our crucified Lord Jesus Christ, to the fruitful purity of the most blessed and most glorious Mary ever Virgin, and to the company of all the Saints; and may we obtain the remission of all our sins through all eternity. (All) Amen.

V. (Presider) Blessed be the womb of the Virgin Mary that bore the Son of the eternal Father.

R. (All) And blessed be the paps that gave suck to Christ our Lord. Amen.

Our Father...

Hail Mary...

Vespers

Traditionally, Vespers is the first office of the liturgical day. It was prayed in religious communities late in the afternoon, along with Compline. Today, it may be of more benefit for the laity to pray it at around 6 in the evening.

Kneel
O divine and adorable Lord Jesus Christ, who has graciously redeemed us by thy bitter passion and death, we offer up these Vespers to thy honor and glory, and most humbly beseech thee, through thy dolorous agony and bloody sweat which thou didst suffer in the garden, to grant us true contrition of heart, and sorrow for our sins, with a firm resolution never more to offend thee, but so satisfy thy divine justice for past iniquity. Amen.

When prayed with others, the Presider taps to call everyone to prayer. Beginning with the Sign of the Cross, the Presider intones and all pray the Hail Mary in silence.

Stand
(Presider) + **Hail, Mary**, full of grace, the Lord is with thee. Blessed art thou among women, and blessed is the fruit of thy womb, Jesus. Holy Mary, Mother of God, pray for us sinners, now and in the hour of our death. Amen.

V. (Presider) Incline unto my aid, + O God.

R. (All) O Lord, make haste to help me.

(Profound bow) Glory be to the Father, and to the Son, and to the Holy Ghost. *As it was in the beginning, is now, and ever shall be, world without end. Amen, Alleluia.

From Vespers on Saturday before Septuagesima Sunday till None on Easter Saturday, instead of Alleluia is said:

Praise be to thee, O Lord, king of eternal glory.

Anthem
The first Cantor stands and recites the appropriate Anthem and the first half line of the Psalm; the second Choir takes up the second half of the line, then the Choirs alternate

(Through the year) While the king was on his couch, my perfumes sent forth an odor of sweetness.

(In Advent) The angel Gabriel was sent to the Virgin Mary, espoused to Joseph, Hail Mary, full of grace, the Lord is with thee. Blessed art thou amongst women. *Alleluia.*

(Christmas time) O admirable intercourse! The Creator of mankind, assuming a body animated with a soul, was pleased to be born of a Virgin, and becoming man without human concurrence, he made us partakers of his divine nature.

Psalm 110

The Messiah, King and Priest, victorious over His enemies

The Lord said to my Lord, "Sit thou on my right hand until I make thy enemies thy footstool." *The Lord shall send forth the scepter of thy power out of Sion, rule thou in the midst of thy enemies.

Thine shall be sovereignty in the day of thy might, in the brightness of the Saints, *from the womb before the daystar I begot thee.

The Lord hath sworn, and he will not repent, "Thou art a priest forever according to the order of Melchisedech."*The Lord on thy right hand has subdued kings in the day of his wrath.

He shall judge the nations, he shall fill ruins. He shall crush heads in the land of many. *Of the brook he shall drink in the way, therefore shall he raise up his head.

(Profound bow) Glory be to the Father, and to the Son, and to the Holy Ghost. *As it was in the beginning, is now, and ever shall be, world without end. Amen.

Cantor

(Through the year) While the king was on his couch, my perfumes sent forth an odor of sweetness.

(In Advent) The angel Gabriel was sent to the Virgin Mary, espoused to Joseph.

(Christmas time) O admirable intercourse! The Creator of mankind, assuming a body animated with a soul, was pleased to be born of a Virgin; and becoming man without human concurrence, he made us partakers of his divine nature.

Vespers

Anthem
The next Cantor stands and recites the Anthem, etc.

(Through the year) His left hand under my head, and his right hand shall embrace me.

(In Advent) Hail Mary, full of grace, the Lord is with thee, blessed art thou amongst women. *Alleluia.*

(Christmas time) When thou wast born after an ineffable manner, the Scriptures were then fulfilled, thou didst descend like rain upon a fleece, to save mankind. O our God, we give thee praise.

Psalm 113
Glory to God, so infinitely great and so admirably condescending

Praise the Lord, ye servants of the Lord, *praise ye the name of the Lord.

Let the name of the Lord be blessed, now and forevermore. *From the rising of the sun to the setting thereof, worthy of praise is the name of the Lord.

High is the Lord above all nations, and above the heavens is his glory. *Who is like unto the Lord our God, who dwelleth on high, and regardeth what is humble in heaven and on earth?

Raising up the needy one from the earth, and from the dunghill lifting up the poor one, to place him with the princes, with the princes of his people. *Who maketh the barren woman to dwell in her house, the joyful mother of many children.

(Profound bow) Glory be to the Father, and to the Son, and to the Holy Ghost. *As it was in the beginning, is now, and ever shall be, world without end. Amen, *Alleluia.*
Cantor

(Through the year) His left hand under my head, and his right hand shall embrace me.

(In Advent) Hail Mary, full of grace, the Lord is with thee, blessed art thou amongst women. *Alleluia.*

(Christmas time) When thou wast born after an ineffable manner, the Scriptures were then fulfilled, thou didst descend like rain upon a fleece, to save mankind. O our God, we give thee praise.

Anthem

The next Cantor stands and recites the Anthem, etc.

(Through the year) I am black but beautiful, O ye daughters of Jerusalem, therefore hath the king loved me and brought me into his chamber.

(In Advent) Do not fear, Mary, thou hast found grace with the Lord. Behold thou shalt conceive, and bring forth a Son.

(Christmas time) In the bush which Moses saw burn without consuming, we acknowledge the preservation of thy glorious virginity. O Mother of God, make intercession for us.

Psalm 122

Song of the pilgrims in honor of Jerusalem

I rejoiced in what hath been told me, "We are to go up to the house of the Lord." *Our feet have stood in thy courts, O Jerusalem, Jerusalem, which is now building like a city, all whose parts are joined together.

For thither the tribes went up, the tribes of the Lord according to the ordinances given to Israel, *to praise the name of the Lord, for there were placed the judgment-seats, the judgment-seats over the house of David.

Ask for what tends to the peace of Jerusalem, and may plenty be to all who love thee. May peace be in thy strength; and plenty within thy walls, *For the sake of my brethren and of my neighbors, I have advocated thy peace. For the sake of the house of the Lord, our God, I have sought good things for thee.

(Profound bow) Glory be to the Father, and to the Son, and to the Holy Ghost. *As it was in the beginning, is now, and ever shall be, world without end. Amen, *Alleluia.*

Cantor

(Through the year) I am black but beautiful, O ye daughters of Jerusalem, therefore hath the king loved me and brought me into his chamber.

(In Advent) Do not fear, Mary, thou hast found grace with the Lord. Behold thou shalt conceive, and bring forth a Son.

(Christmas time) In the bush which Moses saw burn without consuming, we acknowledge the preservation of thy glorious virginity. O Mother of God, make intercession for us.

Anthem
The next Cantor stands and recites the Anthem, etc.

(Through the year) The winter is now past, the rain is over and gone, arise, my love and come.

(In Advent) The Lord will give him the throne of David, his father, and he shall reign forever.

(Christmas time) The root of Jesse hath budded forth, a star hath arisen out of Jacob, a Virgin hath brought forth the Savior: we give thee praise, O our God.

Psalm 127
Man can do nothing without God's help

Unless the Lord himself shall build up the house, in vain have labored the builders thereof, *unless the Lord shall guard the city, in vain watcheth the sentinel thereof.

It is in vain for you to rise before the light. Arise after you have taken rest, you who eat the bread of sorrow. *Since he will give sleep to his beloved ones.

Behold, children are an inheritance from the Lord, the fruit of the womb is a reward. *Like arrows in the hand of a man of power, so shall be the children of those who have been rejected.

Blessed is the man whose quiver is filled with them, *he shall not be confounded when he shall speak to his enemies at the gate.

(Profound bow) Glory be to the Father, and to the Son, and to the Holy Ghost. *As it was in the beginning, is now, and ever shall be, world without end. Amen, *Alleluia.*

(Through the year) The winter is now past, the rain is over and gone, arise, my love and come.

(In Advent) The Lord will give him the throne of David, his father, and he shall reign forever.

(Christmas time) The root of Jesse hath budded forth, a star hath arisen out of Jacob, a Virgin hath brought forth the Savior, we give thee praise, O our God.

Anthem
The next Cantor stands and recites the Anthem, etc.

(Through the year) Thou art become beautiful and sweet, in thy delights, O holy Mother of God.

(In Advent) Behold the handmaid of the Lord, be it done to me according to thy word.

(Christmas time) Behold, Mary hath borne us the Savior, whom John seeing, exclaimed, Behold the Lamb of God, behold him who taketh away the sins of the world, *alleluia.*

Psalm 147
Thanksgiving for the restoration of Jerusalem

O Jerusalem, praise the Lord, *Praise thy God, O Sion.

For strong hath he made the bolts of thy gates, *he hath blessed thy children within thy walls.

It is he who hath settled peace within thy borders, *with the finest flour of wheat he feedeth thee.

'Tis he who sends forth his orders to the earth, *his orders go with speed.

'Tis he who sendeth snow like flocks of wool, *he sprinkleth his hoarfrost like ashes.

He sendeth down his hail like mouthfuls, *who can stand the cold thereof?

He will send forth his word, which shall melt it away, *his spirit shall breathe, and the waters shall flow again.

'Tis he who maketh known his commandments to Jacob, *his law and ordinances to Israel.

He hath not done thus to every nation, *nor hath he made known his law to them.

(Profound bow) Glory be to the Father, and to the Son, and to the Holy Ghost, *As it was in the beginning, is now, and ever shall be, world without end. Amen, *Alleluia.*

(Through the year) Thou art become beautiful and sweet, in thy delights, O holy Mother of God.

(In Advent) Behold the handmaid of the Lord, be it done to me according to thy word.

(Christmas time) Behold, Mary hath borne us the Savior, whom John seeing, exclaimed, Behold the Lamb of God, behold him who taketh away the sins of the world, *alleluia.*

The Little Chapter through the year, except in Advent

Stand

Sirach 24: 9-10

V. (Presider) From the beginning, and before all ages, was I created, and I shall not cease to be in the world to come; and I have ministered before him in his holy abode.

R. (All) Thanks be to God.

The Little Chapter In Advent

Isaiah 11: 1-2

V. (Presider) There shall come forth a rod out of the root of Jesse, and a flower shall spring out of its root, and the Spirit of the Lord shall rest upon him.

R. (All) Thanks be to God.

Kneel during the first four verses of the Ave Maris Stella.

The first Cantor begins the hymn, and his Choir continues it; the second strophe is said by the opposite Choir, and so on. At the last strophe, both Choirs combine, and bow profoundly

Bright Mother of Our Maker, Hail

Ave Maris Stella

Bright Mother of our Ma - ker, hail!
Thou Vir - gin e - ver blest,
The'o - cean's star by which, we sail,
and gain the port of rest.

Release our long en - tan - gled mind,
from all the snares of ill,
With heavenly light ins - truct the blind,
and all our vows ful - fill.

O'spot - less maid, whose vir - tues shine,
from all sus - pi - cion free,
Each'Ac - tion of our lives re - fine,
and make us pure like thee.

While'we this hail, ad - dressed to thee,
Exert for us a mo - ther's care,
Preserve our lives uns - tainded with ill,

from Ga - briel's mouth re - hearse,
and us thy chil - dren own,
in this in - fec - ted way,

obtain that peace our lot may be,
prevail with him to hear our prayer,
that heaven a - lone our souls may fill,

and E - va's name re - verse.
who chose to by thy Son.
with joys that ne'er de - cay. A - men.

Final verse:

(Profound bow) To God the Father endless praise;
To God the Son the same,
And Holy Ghost whose equal rays,
One equal glory claim. Amen.

V. (Cantors) Grace is spread on thy lips.
R. (All) Therefore God hath blessed thee forever.

Ave Maris Stella

With permission of the copyright holder
https://www.youtube.com/watch?v=nCzQ-wB6Ecc

V. (Cantors) Grace is spread on thy lips.
R. (All) Therefore God hath blessed thee forever.

Anthem

The next Cantor stands and recites the Anthem, etc.

(Through the year) O blessed Mother, and chaste virgin, glorious queen of the world, make intercession for us to the Lord.

(Easter time) O Queen of Heaven, rejoice, *Alleluia*. Because He whom thou didst deserve to bear, *Alleluia*, is risen again, as he foretold, *Alleluia*. Pray for us to God, *Alleluia*.

(In Advent) The Holy Ghost shall come upon thee, Mary. Do not fear, thou shalt have in thy womb the Son of God, *Alleluia*.

(Christmas time) Great is the mystery of our inheritance, the womb of a pure virgin became the temple of God. He who took flesh of her was not defiled. All nations shall come and say, "Glory be to thee, O Lord."

The Magnificat
Luke 1: 46-55

Stand

My soul doth magnify the Lord, *and my spirit hath rejoiced in God my Savior.

Because he hath regarded the humility of his handmaid, *behold from henceforth all generations shall call me blessed.

For he who is mighty hath done great things to me, *and holy is his name.

And his mercy is from generation to generation, *to them who fear him.

He hath shown might in his arm, *he hath scattered the proud in the conceit of their heart.

He hath cast down the mighty from their seats, *and hath exalted the humble.

He hath filled the hungry with good things, *and the rich he hath sent away empty.

He hath received Israel his servant, being mindful of his mercy, *as he spoke to our Fathers; to Abraham and to his seed forever.

(Profound bow) Glory be to the Father, and to the Son, and to the Holy Ghost, *As it was in the beginning, is now, and ever shall be, world without end. Amen, *Alleluia*.

Cantor

(Through the year) O blessed Mother, and chaste virgin, glorious queen of the world, make intercession for us to the Lord.

21

(Easter time) O Queen of Heaven, rejoice, *Alleluia*. Because He whom thou didst deserve to bear, *Alleluia*, is risen again, as he foretold, *Alleluia*. Pray for us to God, *Alleluia*.

(In Advent) The Holy Ghost shall come upon thee, Mary. Do not fear, thou shalt have in thy womb the Son of God, *Alleluia*.

(Christmas time) Great is the mystery of our inheritance, the womb of a pure virgin became the temple of God. He who took flesh of her was not defiled. All nations shall come and say, "Glory be to thee, O Lord."

(First Choir) Lord, have mercy on us.

(Second Choir) Christ, have mercy on us.

(All) Lord, have mercy on us.

V. (Cantors) O Lord, hear my prayer.

R. (All) And let my cry come unto thee.

Let us pray
Presider stands and prays

(Through the year) Grant, we beseech thee, O Lord God, that we, thy servants, may enjoy constant health of mind and body; and by the glorious intercession of the ever blessed Virgin Mary, may be delivered from all temporal afflictions, and enjoy eternal bliss. Through Christ, our Lord.

R. (All) Amen.

(In Advent) O God, who was pleased that thy eternal word, when the angel delivered his message, should take flesh in the womb of the blessed Virgin Mary; give ear to our humble petitions, and grant that we, who believe her to be truly the mother of God, may be assisted by her prayers. Through the same Christ our Lord.

R. (All) Amen.

(Christmas time) O God, who by the fruitful virginity of the Blessed Virgin Mary, has given to mankind the rewards of eternal salvation; grant, we beseech thee, that we may experience her intercession, by whom we have received the author of life, our Lord Jesus Christ thy Son.

R. (All) Amen.

Commemoration of the Saints
Through the year, except Advent

(All) All ye saints of God, vouchsafe to make intercession for the salvation of us and of all mankind.

V. (Cantors) Rejoice in the Lord, ye just and be exceedingly glad.

R. (All) And exult in glory, all ye upright of heart.

Let us pray

(Presider) Protect, O Lord, thy people, and grant us thy continual assistance, which we humbly beg with confidence, through the intercession of St. Peter and St. Paul, and of thy other Apostles. May all thy Saints, we beseech thee, O Lord, always assist our weakness, that whilst we celebrate their merits, we may experience their protection. Grant us thy peace in our days, and banish all evils from thy Church. Prosperously guide the steps, actions, and desires of us, and of all thy servants, in the way of salvation. Give eternal blessings to our benefactors, and grant everlasting rest to all the faithful departed. Through our Lord Jesus Christ, thy Son, who liveth and reigneth with thee and the Holy Ghost, one God, world without end.

R. (All) Amen.

Commemoration of the Saints in Advent

(All) Behold, the Lord will come, and all his Saints with him, and there shall be a great light on that day, *Alleluia.*

V. (Cantor) Behold, the Lord shall appear on a bright cloud.

R. (All) And with him thousands of Saints.

Let us pray

(Presider) Cleanse our consciences, we beseech thee, O Lord, by thy holy visit, that when Jesus Christ, thy Son, our Lord, cometh with all his Saints, he may find in us an abode prepared for his reception: who liveth and reigneth with thee and the Holy Ghost, one God, world without end.

R. (All) Amen.

V. (Cantor) O Lord, hear my prayer

R. (All) And let my cry come unto thee.

V. (Cantors) Let us bless the Lord.

R. (All) Thanks be to God.

V. (Presider) May the souls of the faithful departed, through the mercy of God, rest in peace.

R. (All) Amen.

Compline

*Said in the evening, for the laity normally before going to
bed. A short office, by it we prepare our souls for death.*

Kneel

*(Silently) O divine and adorable Lord Jesus Christ, who has graciously
redeemed us by thy bitter passion and death, we offer up this Compline to thy
honor and glory, and most humbly beseech thee, through the injury thou didst
suffer by the treacherous kiss of Judas, and by thy capture in the garden, to
grant us thy grace that we may never betray thee by unworthily receiving the
blessed sacraments, particularly the adorable Eucharist of thy body and
blood, in the state of mortal sin, and that we may bridle our passions, and
bind down our vicious inclinations under the sweet yoke and light burden of
thy holy law till death. Amen.*

The Presider calls everyone to prayer. Beginning with
the Sign of the Cross, the Presider intoning, all pray the
Hail Mary in silence

Stand

(Presider) + **Hail, Mary**, full of grace, the Lord is with thee.
Blessed art thou among women, and blessed is the fruit of thy
womb, Jesus. Holy Mary, mother of God, pray for us sinners, now
and in the hour of our death. **Amen.**

V. (Presider) Convert us to thee, O God, our Savior.

R. (All) And turn away thy wrath from us.

V. (Presider) Incline unto my aid, + O God.

R. (All) O Lord, make haste to help me.

(Profound bow) Glory be to the Father, and to the Son, and to
the Holy Ghost. *As it was in the beginning, is now, and ever shall
be, world without end. Amen, *Alleluia.*

*From Vespers on Saturday before the ninth Sunday before
Easter (Septuagesima Sunday) till None on the Saturday
after Easter, instead of Alleluia is said:*

Praise be to thee, O Lord, king of eternal glory.

*The first Cantor stands and recites the first half line of the
Psalm; the second Choir takes up the second half of the
line, then the Choirs alternate*

Psalm 129

Confidence in God; the persecutors of the Church come to nothing

Many times have they fought against me from my youth, *let
Israel now say.

(Sit) Many times have they fought against me from my youth,
*but they could not prevail over me.

The wicked have exerted their cruelty upon my back, *they
have prolonged their iniquity.

The Lord, who is just, will cut the neck of sinners, *let them
all be confounded and rejected who hate Sion.

Let them be as grass upon the tops of houses, *which withered
away before it was plucked up.

Wherewith the mower did not fill his hand, *nor the gleaner
his bosom.

And they who passed by have not said, "The blessing of the
Lord be upon you." *We have blessed you in the name of the
Lord.

(Profound bow) Glory be to the Father, and to the Son, and to
the Holy Ghost. *As it was in the beginning, is now, and ever shall
be, world without end. Amen. *Alleluia.*

Psalm 130

Prayer of a sinner trusting in the mercies of God

From the deep I have cried out to thee, *O gracious Lord, hear
my voice.

Let thy ears be attentive, *to the voice of my petition.

If thou wilt consider our iniquities, O mighty Lord, *who shall
endure it?

But with thee there is merciful forgiveness, *and by reason of
thy law I have waited on thee, O Lord.

My soul hath relied on his word, *my soul hath hoped in the
Lord.

From the morning watch even until night, *let Israel hope in
the Lord.

Because with the Lord there is mercy, *and with him plentiful
redemption.

And he shall redeem Israel *from all his iniquities.

(Profound bow) Glory be to the Father, and to the Son, and to the Holy Ghost, *as it was in the beginning, is now, and ever shall be, world without end. Amen, *Alleluia.*

Psalm 131

A psalm of childlike resignation to God's will

O Lord, my heart is not puffed up, *nor are my eyes disdainful.

Neither have I been ambitious of great affairs, *nor have I dared to scrutinize in wonderful things above me.

If I thought not humbly of myself, *but proudly elevated my mind,

Treat me as a nurse treats her infant, *when she weans it from her breasts.

Let Israel hope in the Lord, *now and forevermore.

(Profound bow) Glory be to the Father, and to the Son, and to the Holy Ghost, *As it was in the beginning, is now, and ever shall be, world without end. Amen, *Alleluia.*

The first Cantor begins the hymn, and his Choir continues it; the second strophe is said by the opposite Choir, and so on. At the last strophe, both Choirs combine, and bow profoundly

Remember Thou Creator Lord

Memento, rerum Conditor

Memento Rerum Conditor

Me- men - to, re - rum Con - di- tor, nos-
Ma - ri - a Ma - ter gra - ti- ae, Dul-
Je - su ti - bi sit glo - ri - a, qui

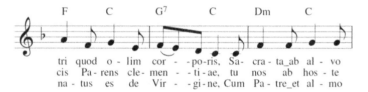

tri quod o - lim cor - -po-ris, Sa - cra - ta_ab al - vo
cis Pa - rens cle - men - -ti- ae, tu nos ab hos - te
na - tus es de Vir - -gi- ne, Cum Pa- tre_et al - mo

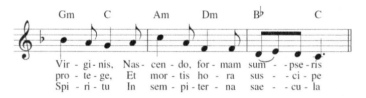

Vir - gi- nis, Nas - cen - do, for - mam sum - -pse-ris
pro - te - ge, Et mor - tis ho - ra sus - -ci- pe
Spi - ri- tu In sem - pi- ter - na sae - -cu - la

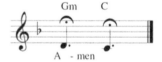

A - men

São Pedro Partituras - 2017
saopedropartituras.blogspot.com

The Little Chapter through the year, except in Advent

Sirach 24: 24
Douay Rheims 1899 American Edition (DRA)

(Presider) I am the mother of beautiful love, and of fear, and of knowledge, and of holy hope.

R. (All) Thanks be to God.

V. (Presider) Pray for us, O holy Mother of God.

R. (All) That we may be made worthy of the promises of Christ.

The Little Chapter in Advent

Isaiah 7:14

(Presider) Behold, a virgin shall conceive and bring forth a Son, and his name shall be called Emmanuel. He shall eat butter and honey, that he may know how to reject evil and choose good.

R. (All) Thanks be to God.

V. (Presider) The angel of the Lord declared unto Mary

R. (All) And she conceived by the Holy Ghost.

Anthem
The Cantor stands and prays

(Through the year) Under thy protection we seek refuge, O holy Mother of God; despise not our petitions in our necessities, but deliver us continually from all dangers, O glorious and blessed Virgin.

(Paschal time) O Queen of Heaven, rejoice, *Alleluia*, because he whom thou didst deserve to bear, *Alleluia*, is risen again, as he foretold, *Alleluia*: pray for us to God, *Alleluia*.

(In Advent) The Holy Ghost shall come upon thee, Mary: do not fear, thou shalt have in thy womb the Son of God, alleluia.

(Christmas time) Great is the mystery of our inheritance: the womb of a pure virgin became the temple of God: he, who took flesh of her, was not defiled: all nations shall come and say: Glory be to thee, O Lord.

Canticle of Simeon
Luke 2:29-32

Now dost thou dismiss thy servant, O Lord, *according to thy word, in peace.

Since my eyes have seen *thy promised salvation.

Which thou hast prepared *to show to all nations;

A light to enlighten the Gentiles, *and the glory of thy people Israel.

(Through the year) Under thy protection we seek refuge, O holy Mother of God; despise not our petitions in our necessities, but deliver us continually from all dangers, O glorious and blessed virgin.

(Paschal time) O Queen of Heaven, rejoice, *Alleluia*, because he whom thou didst deserve to bear, *Alleluia*, is risen again, as he foretold, *Alleluia*: pray for us to God, *Alleluia*.

(In Advent) The Holy Ghost shall come upon thee, Mary: do not fear, thou shalt have in thy womb the Son of God, alleluia.

(Christmas time) Great is the mystery of our inheritance: the womb of a pure virgin became the temple of God: He, who took flesh of her, was not defiled: all nations shall come and say: Glory be to thee, O Lord.

(First Choir) Lord have mercy on us.

(Second Choir) Christ, have mercy on us.

(All) Lord, have mercy on us.

V. (Cantors) O Lord, hear my prayer.

R. (All) And let my cry come unto thee.

Let us pray
Presider

(Through the year) Grant, we beseech thee, O Lord, that the glorious intercession of the ever blessed and glorious Virgin Mary may protect us here, and bring us to everlasting life. Through our Lord Jesus Christ, thy Son: Who with thee and the Holy Ghost, liveth and reigneth one God, world without end.

R. (All) Amen.

(In Advent) O God, who was pleased that thy Word, when the angel delivered his message, should take flesh in the womb of the blessed Virgin Mary; give ear to our humble petitions, and grant that we, who believe her to be truly the mother of God, may be helped by her prayers. Through the same Lord Jesus Christ, who with thee and the Holy Ghost liveth and reigneth one God, world without end.

R. (All) Amen.

(Christmas time) O God, who, by the fruitful virginity of

blessed Mary, has given to mankind the rewards of eternal salvation; grant, we beseech thee, that we may experience her intercession, by whom we have deserved to receive the Author of life, our Lord Jesus Christ, thy Son: Who with thee and the Holy Ghost, liveth and reigneth one God, world without end.

R. (All) Amen.

V. (Cantors) O Lord, hear my prayer.

R. (All) And let my cry come unto thee.

V. (Cantors) Let us bless the Lord.

R. (All) Thanks be to God.

Blessing

(Presider) May the almighty and merciful Lord, + the Father, the Son, and the Holy Ghost, bless and protect us.

R. (All) Amen.

Then should be sung one of the great Anthems of the Blessed Virgin Mary, according to the time of year. Prayed kneeling

Marian Anthems

From Advent to the Purification

MOTHER OF JESUS

Alma Redemptoris Mater,

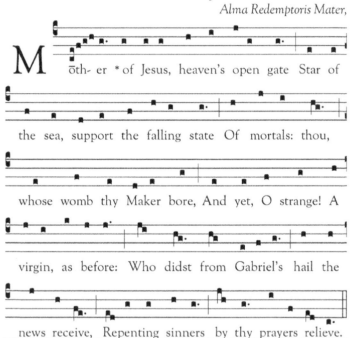

Moth- er * of Jesus, heaven's open gate Star of

the sea, support the falling state Of mortals: thou,

whose womb thy Maker bore, And yet, O strange! A

virgin, as before: Who didst from Gabriel's hail the

news receive, Repenting sinners by thy prayers relieve.

Sao Pedro Partituras – 2019
saopedropartituras.blogspot.com
Used with permission of the copyright holder

From Advent to the Purification
Alma Redemptoris Mater

Ant. 5.

A L- ma * Redemptó-ris Ma-ter, quæ pérvi- a

cǽli porta manes, Et stella ma-ris, succúrre cadénti

súrge-re qui cu-rat pópu-lo : Tu quæ genu- ísti,

na-tú-ra mi-ránte, tu- um sanctum Ge-ni-tó-rem:

Virgo pri- us ac posté-ri- us, Gabri- é-lis ab o-re

sumens illud Ave, pecca-tó-rum mi-se-ré-re.

Let us pray.

(Presider) Pour forth, we beseech thee, O Lord, thy grace into our hearts, that we, to whom the incarnation of Christ, thy Son, was made known by the message of an angel, may by his passion and cross be brought to the glory of this resurrection: through the same Christ our Lord.

R. (All) Amen.

From Christmas Eve, the above Versicles and Prayer are changed thus:

V. (Cantors) After childbirth thou didst remain a pure virgin.

R. (All) O Mother of God, intercede for us.

Let us pray

(Presider) O God, who by the fruitful virginity of blessed Mary, has given to mankind the rewards of eternal salvation; grant, we beseech thee, that we may experience her intercession, by whom we receive the Author of life, our Lord Jesus Christ, thy Son. Amen.

From The Purification until Holy Saturday

HAIL MARY, QUEEN OF HEAVENLY SPHERES!

Ave Regina Cælorum

Hail Mary, Queen of heavenly spheres! * Hail, whom th'an-gelic host reveres Hail, fruitful root! Hail, sacred gate! From whom our light derives its date. O glorious Maid, with beauty blest! May joys eternal fill thy breast! Thus crowned with beauty and with joy, Thy prayers for us with Christ employ.

Sao Pedro Partituras – 2019
saopedropartituras.blogspot.com

Ave Regina Caelorum

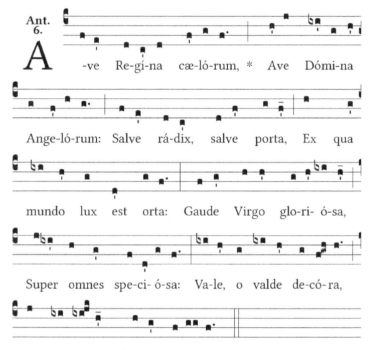

Ant. 6.

A -ve Re-gí-na cæ-ló-rum, * Ave Dómi-na

Ange-ló-rum: Salve rá-dix, salve porta, Ex qua

mundo lux est orta: Gaude Virgo glo-ri- ó-sa,

Super omnes spe-ci- ó-sa: Va-le, o valde de-có- ra,

Et pro no-bis Christum exó- ra.

V. (Cantors) Vouchsafe, O sacred Virgin, to accept my praises.

R. (All) Give me strength against thy enemies.

Let us pray

V. (Presider) Grant us, O merciful God, strength against all our weakness; that we, who celebrate the memory of the holy Mother of God, may by the help of her intercession rise again from our iniquities: through the same Christ, our Lord.

R. (All) Amen.

From Easter through the Saturday of the week following Pentecost, which is sometimes called Whitsun Week.

REJOICE, O QUEEN OF HEAVEN

Regina Cæli

Rejoice, O Queen of heaven, * to see, al-le-luia,

The sa-cred infant born of thee, al-le-luia, Return in

glory from the tomb, al-le- luia: And with thy prayers

prevent our doom, al-le-lu-ia.

Regina Caeli

Ant. 6.

R E-gí-na cǽli * læ-tá-re, alle-lú-ia : Qui-a

quem me-ru-ísti portá-re, alle-lú-ia : Re-surréx-it,

si-cut dix-it, alle-lú-ia : Ora pro no-bis De-um,

alle-lú- ia.

Let us pray

V. (Presider) O God, who by the resurrection of thy Son, our Lord Jesus Christ, has been pleased to fill the world with joy; grant, we beseech thee, that by the intercession of the Virgin Mary, his mother, we may receive the joys of eternal life: through the same Christ, our Lord.

R. Amen.

From Trinity Sunday eve to the beginning of Advent

HAIL, HAPPY QUEEN

Salve Regina

Hail, happy Queen * thou mercy's parent, hail! : life, hope, and comfort , of this earthly va-le. To thee we, Eva's wretched children, cry, In sighs and tears, to thee suppliants fly. Rise, glorious advocate, exert thy love, And let our vows- those eyes of pity move. O pious Virgin Mary, grant that we,- Long exiled, may in heaven thy Jesus see. O cle-ment, O loving, O sweet Vir-gin Mary.

Salve Regina

Alve, Re-gí-na, * má-ter mi-se-ri-córdi- æ :

Ví-ta, dulcé- do, et spes nóstra, sálve. Ad te cla-

mámus, éxsu-les, fí-li- i Hévæ. Ad te suspi-rámus,

geméntes et fléntes in hac lacrimá-rum válle.

E-ia ergo, Advo-cá-ta nóstra, íl-los tú-os mi-se-

ri-córdes ócu-los ad nos convérte. Et Jé-sum,

bene-díctum frúctum véntris tú- i, no-bis post hoc

exsí-li- um osténde. O clé- mens : O pí- a :

O dúlcis * Virgo Ma-rí- a.

V. Pray for us, O holy mother of God.

R. That we may be made worthy of the promises of Christ.

Let us pray

V. (Presider) O Almighty and eternal God, who by the cooperation of the Holy Ghost, didst prepare the body and soul of the glorious Virgin Mary, that she might become a habitation worthy of thy Son; grant that, as with joy we celebrate her memory, so by her pious intercession we may be delivered form present evils and eternal death: Through the same Christ, our Lord.

R. (All) Amen.

After the proper Anthem of the Blessed Virgin Mary, according to the time of year, is said the Versicle:

V. (Cantors) May the divine assistance always remain with us.

R. (All) Amen.

Compline terminates with the following prayers:

Our Father, who art in heaven, hallowed be thy name. Thy kingdom come, thy will be done on earth as it is in heaven. Give us this day our daily bread, and forgive us our trespasses as we forgive them who trespass against us. And lead us not into temptation, but deliver us from evil. Amen.

Hail Mary full of grace, the Lord is with thee. Blessed art thou among women, and blessed is the fruit of thy womb, Jesus. Holy Mary, mother of God, pray for us sinners, now and at the hour of our death. Amen.

I believe in God, the Father almighty, creator of heaven and earth. And in Jesus Christ, his only Son, our Lord, who was conceived by the Holy Ghost, born of the Virgin Mary, suffered under Pontius Pilate, was crucified, dead and buried. He ascended into heaven, sitteth at the right hand of God, the Father almighty. From thence he will come to judge the living and the dead. I believe in the Holy Ghost, the holy Catholic Church, the communion of saints, the forgiveness of sins, the resurrection of the body, and life everlasting. Amen.

Note: If Matins is recited immediately after Compline, the Prayers After the Office should not be said till after Lauds.

Matins & Lauds

Being "nocturns" these two hours were traditionally recited at night, closer to midnight than to dawn, often due to the divisions of the monastic day. The laity will find in their character an anticipation of the sunrise, and should take that same attitude in prayer. These are now most often prayed in the morning.

Matins

Kneel

(Silently) *O Divine and adorable Lord Jesus Christ, who have graciously redeemed us by your bitter passion and death, we offer up these Matins and Lauds to your honor and glory, and most humbly beseech you, through the vile treatment you received from the Jews, who dragged you to the courts of impious High priests, where you were falsely accused, struck in the face, called a blasphemer, and declared guilty of death, and suffered most cruel torments with blows, bruises, and unheard-of injuries, during the whole night, to grant us resignation and silence during all calumnies, detractions, and sufferings for the love of you, and to give us grace never to return injury for injury, but to practice that truly Christian revenge of overcoming evil with good, to do good to those who hate us, to bless those who curse us, and to pray for those who persecute and calumniate us: Amen.*

The Presider calls everyone to prayer. Beginning with the Sign of the Cross, intoned by the Presider, all pray the Hail Mary in silence.

Stand

+ **Hail Mary**, full of grace, the Lord is with thee. Blessed art thou amongst women and blessed is the fruit of thy womb, Jesus. Holy Mary, Mother of God, pray for us sinners, now and at the hour of our death. Amen.

V. (Presider) O Lord, + open thou my lips.

R. (All) And my mouth shall declare thy praise

V. (Presider) Incline unto my aid, + O God.

R. (All) O Lord, make haste to help me.

(Profound bow) Glory be to the Father, and to the Son, and to the Holy Ghost. *As it was in the beginning, is now, and ever shall

42

be, world without end. Amen, *Alleluia.*

From Vespers on Saturday before the ninth Sunday before Easter (Septuagesima Sunday) till None on the Saturday after Easter, instead of Alleluia is said:

Praise be to thee, O Lord, king of eternal glory.

Invitatory

(Cantors) Hail Mary full of grace, the Lord is with thee.
(Choirs) Hail Mary full of grace, the Lord is with thee.

Psalm 95
An invitation to praise God, and to obey Him

(Cantors) Come, let us rejoice in the Lord, let us joyfully cry out to God our Savior. Let us present ourselves before him to celebrate his praises, and to sing with joy canticles unto him.

(Choirs) Hail, Mary, full of grace, the Lord is with thee.

(Cantors) Because God is a mighty Lord and a great King above all gods; for the Lord will not reject his people; in his hand are all the bounds of the earth, and he looks down on the heights of the mountains.

(Choirs) The Lord is with thee.

(Cantors) The sea is his; for he made it, and his hands framed the earth. (All kneel) Come then, let us adore, and fall prostrate before God, let us weep in the presence of the Lord who made us, because he is the Lord our God; We are his people, and the sheep of his pasture. (Rise)

(Choirs) Hail, Mary, full of grace, the Lord is with thee.

(Cantors) If this day you should hear his voice, harden not your hearts as you did when you provoked him, on the day you offended him in the desert; where your fathers tempted me, they tried and saw my works.

(Choirs) The Lord is with thee.

(Cantors) I was forty years with this race of men, and said: The hearts of this people are always wandering, but they have not known my ways, and I swore to them in my wrath, that they should not enter my abode of rest.

(Choirs) Hail, Mary, full of grace, the Lord is with thee.

(Cantors, with all bowing) Glory be to the Father, and to the Son, and to the Holy Ghost. As it was in the beginning, is now, and ever shall be, world without end. Amen. *(Rise)*
The Lord is with thee.
(Cantors) Hail, Mary, full of grace, the Lord is with thee.

The first Cantor begins the hymn and his Choir continues it; the second strophe is said by the opposite Choir, and so on. At the last strophe, both Choirs combine, and bow profoundly

O Sovereign God

Quem terra pontus sidera

O so-vereign God whose hands sus-tain, the
He, whom the Sun and Moon o-bey, to
O Hap-py Ma-ry, chose to bear, thy
The an-gel's voice pro-nounced thee blest, the
To thee, o Je-sus, Ma-ry's Son, be

globe of heaven the earth and main, a-
whom all crea-tures' ho-mage pay, the
Ma-ker's co-e-ter-nal Heir; Whose
Ho-ly Ghost on thee did rest, to
e-ver-las-ting ho-mage done; To

dored and praised by each de-gree, lies
Judge of man and An-gels' doom, Re-
fin-gers span this earth a-round, whose
us thou didst bes-tow by birth, the
God the Fath-er we re-peat the

hid, o Sa--cred Maid in thee.
sides wi-thin thy Vir-gin womb.
arms the whole cre-a-tions bound.
most de-sired of heaven and earth.
same, and to the Pa-ra-clete. A-men.

São Pedro Partituras - 2017
saopedropartituras.blogspot.com

With permission of the copyright holder
https://www.youtube.com/watch?v=4jMbZiNi13c

Quem Terra Pontus Sidera

São Pedro Partituras - 2017
saopedropartituras.blogspot.com

With permission of the copyright holder
https://www.youtube.com/watch?v=4jMbZiNi13c

Nocturns
On Sunday, Monday, and Thursday

Anthem

Cantor stands

Blessed art thou among women: and blessed is the fruit of thy womb.

Psalm 8

God is wonderful in His works; especially in mankind, singularly exalted by the Incarnation of Christ

Stand

O Lord, our sovereign Lord, *how wonderful is thy name over the whole earth!

(Sit) For thy grandeur is exalted *above the heavens.

Thou hast received due praise from the mouths of infants and sucklings to confound thy enemies, *and to destroy the spirit of hatred and vengeance.

For I shall consider the heavens, which are the work of thy hands, *the moon and stars, which thou has formed.

What is man, that thou art mindful of him, *or the son of man, that thou dost visit him?

Thou hast created him a little inferior to the angels. *Thou hast crowned him with honor and glory and gave him dominion over all the works of thy hands.

Thou hast rendered all things subject to him, *the sheep, and the oxen, and also the cattle of the field.

The birds of the air and the fishes of the sea, *and all that glide through the course of the waters.

O Lord, our sovereign Lord, *how wonderful is thy name over the whole earth!

(Profound bow) Glory be to the Father, and to the Son, and to the Holy Ghost. *As it was in the beginning, is now, and ever shall be, world without end. Amen.

Anthem: Blessed art thou among women: and blessed is the fruit of thy womb.

Anthem

Cantor stands

Like choice myrrh, thou hast rendered a most fragrant odor, O holy Mother of God.

47

Psalm 19

The works of God show forth His glory

The heavens display the glory of God, *and the firmament publishes the works of his hands.

Each day announces his word to the following day, *and each night declares his knowledge to the succeeding night.

There are no tongues or languages, *where their voices are not heard.

Their eloquence went forth through the whole world, *and their words have reached the bounds of the earth.

The glory of his abode is fulgent like the Sun, *and he is adorned like the bridegroom going out of his chamber.

He proceedeth with joy like a giant on his way, *his coming forth begins from the summit of heaven.

And he continues his course to the end thereof: *there is not one who can abscond from his rays.

The law of the Lord is perfect, it converts souls, *the words of the Lord are faithful, and give wisdom to the humble.

The ordinances of the Lord are righteous, rejoicing the hearts, *the precept of the Lord is luminous, and enlightens our understanding.

The fear of the Lord is holy, and continues forevermore, *the judgments of the Lord are founded on truth and justice.

They are more desirable than gold or precious stones, *and sweeter than the honey and honeycomb.

For thy servant observeth them, *and they who keep them, find an ample recompense.

Who can comprehend what sin is? Cleanse me from my hidden sins, *and from those of others save thy servant.

If they shall not be imputed to me, I will be then pure *and will be free from the very great guilt of sin.

Then shall my prayer be directed to please thee, *and my interior meditation be always made in thy presence.

O Lord, thou art my help *and my Redeemer.

(Profound bow) Glory be to the Father, and to the Son, and to the Holy Ghost. *As it was in the beginning, is now, and ever shall be, world without end. Amen.

Anthem: Like choice myrrh, thou has rendered a most fragrant odor, O holy Mother of God.

Anthem

Cantor stands

In honor of this most chase Virgin let us sing canticles with sweet harmony.

Psalm 24

A song of triumph for the translation of the Ark to Mount Sion

The Lord possesses the earth, and all that it contains: *he owns the whole world and all its inhabitants.

For he hath founded it on the seas, *and hath raised it over the surface of the rivers.

Who shall ascend on the mount of the Lord, *and who shall dwell in his holy sanctuary?

Those who do no harm, and are pure of heart, *who give not their hearts to vain desires, nor deceives his neighbor by false oaths.

He shall receive the blessing of the Lord, *and mercy from God his Savior.

Such is the inheritance of those who truly seek him, *who desire the presence of the God of Jacob.

Open wide your gates, O ye princes, and let the eternal doors be thrown open, *and the King of Glory shall make his entrance.

Who is this King of glory? *He is the valiant and mighty Lord, the Lord who has triumphed in battle.

Open wide your gates, O ye princes, let the eternal gates be thrown open, *and the King of glory shall make his entrance.

Who is this King of glory? *The Lord of hosts is this king of glory.

(Profound bow) Glory be to the Father, and to the Son, and to the Holy Ghost. *As it was in the beginning, is now, and ever shall be, world without end. Amen.

Anthem: In honor of this most chase Virgin, let us sing canticles with sweet harmony.

V. (Cantors) Grace is spread on thy lips.

R. (All) Therefore God has blessed thee forever.

V. (Presider) **Our Father**, (silently)...And lead us not into temptation

R. (All) But deliver us from evil. Amen.

On Tuesday and Friday

Anthem

Cantor stands

In thy comeliness and thy beauty go on, proceed prosperously, and reign.

Psalm 45

Stand

The excellence of Christ's kingdom, and the endowments of His Church

My heart is ready to declare grand things. *I will devote my works to the King of kings.

(Sit) My tongue shall follow his inspiration, *like a quick pen of an able scrivener.

O thou most beautiful among the sons of men, grace is spread on thy lips. *Therefore God hath blessed thee forever.

Gird thyself with thy sword, *O thou most Mighty.

In thy comeliness and thy beauty, *go on, proceed prosperously, and reign.

For the sake of truth, of meekness, and of justice, *and thy right hand shall conduct thee wonderfully.

Thy arrows are sharp, under thee shall people fall. *They shall pierce the hearts of the king's enemies.

Thy throne, O God, is an eternal reign. *The scepter of thy empire is a scepter of equity.

Thou hast loved justice, and hated iniquity, *therefore the Lord thy God anointed thee with the oil of joy above all thy partners.

Myrrh, and aloes, and cassia perfume thy robes, and thy ivory palaces, *where the daughters of the king have the honor to entertain thee.

The queen on thy right hand in vesture trimmed with gold, *and variegated with ornaments.

Hearken, my daughter, and see and incline thy ear, *forget thy people, and thy father's house.

And the king will be enamored with thy beauty, *for he is the Lord thy God, and the people will adore him.

And the daughters of Tyre shall offer gifts, *yea the rich nobility too will come to render thee their vows.

All the glory of the king's daughter is in her interior, *although she be decorated with fringes of gold and embroideries.

Virgins shall be conducted in her retinue to the king. *Her

neighbors shall be brought to thee.

They shall be accompanied with joy and delights, *and shall be introduced into the temple of the king.

Thou art blessed with children to hold the place of thy fathers. *Thou wilt appoint them princes over the whole earth.

They shall be mindful of thy name, *through succession of ages.

Therefore shall the people praise thee forever, *yea for evermore.

(Profound bow) Glory be to the Father, and to the Son, and to the Holy Ghost. *As it was in the beginning, is now, and ever shall be, world without end. Amen.

Anthem: In thy comeliness and thy beauty go on, proceed prosperously, and reign.

Anthem

Cantor stands

God will assist her with his presence. God is in the midst of her; she shall not be disturbed.

Psalm 46

The Church in persecution trusts in the protection of God

God is our refuge and strength, *he is our helper in afflictions, which have heavily fallen on us.

So we shall have nothing to fear when the earth will be troubled, *and the mountains transported into the depth of the sea.

The waters roared, and were disturbed, *and their impetuous torrent made the mountains tremble.

A current of heavenly joy overflows the city of God, *the Most High hath sanctified his own tabernacle.

God is in the midst thereof, it shall not be disturbed, *the Lord will protect it from the dawn of the morning.

Nations are disturbed, and kingdoms have tottered, *the earth trembled at his voice.

The Lord of hosts is with us, *the God of Jacob is our protector.

Come and behold the works of the Lord, and the prodigies he wrought on earth. *He makes the wars cease, even to the bounds of the earth.

He shall destroy the bow, and break the weapons, *and cast

the shields into the fire.

Consider, and know that I am the Lord. *I shall rule over nations, and shall be great on earth.

The Lord of hosts is with us, *the God of Jacob is our protector.

(Profound bow) Glory be to the Father, and to the Son, and to the Holy Ghost. *As it was in the beginning, is now, and ever shall be, world without end. Amen.

Anthem: God will assist her with his presence. God is in the midst of her, she shall not be disturbed.

Anthem
Cantor stands

We all shall truly rejoice, if we are constantly devoted to thee, O holy Mother of God.

Psalm 87
The glory of the Church is Christ

Sion is founded on holy mountains, *the Lord is pleased with its gates above all the tabernacles of Jacob.

Glorious things are spoken of thee, O city of God. *I shall be mindful of Rahab and Babylon, to whom I will make myself known.

Behold the Philistines and Tyre, and the inhabitants of Ethiopia: *these shall be there.

Shall not Sion say: A man is born in her, *and this man is the Most High, who founded her?

The Lord shall relate in the records of the people and of princes, *the names of those who have dwelt therein.

All shall truly rejoice, *who abide in thee.

(Profound bow) Glory be to the Father, and to the Son, and to the Holy Ghost. *As it was in the beginning, is now, and ever shall be, world without end. Amen.

Anthem: We all shall truly rejoice, if we are constantly devoted to thee, O holy Mother of God.

All stand

V. (Cantors) Grace is spread on thy lips.

R. (All) Therefore God has blessed thee forever.

V. (Presider) **Our Father**, (silently)....And lead us not into temptation

R. But deliver us from evil.

52

On Wednesday and Saturday

Anthem

Cantor stands

Rejoice, O Virgin Mary, thou alone has rendered the Church triumphant over all the heresies spread through the earth.

Psalm 96

Stand

An exhortation to all creatures to praise God

Sing to the Lord a new canticle: *let the whole earth chant the praises of the Lord.

(Sit) Sing to the Lord, and bless his holy name: *proclaim each day the good tidings of salvation.

Publish his glory among the Gentiles, *and his wonderful works among the people.

For the Lord is great, and most worthy of all praise: *he is to be feared above all the gods of the earth.

Because all the gods of the Gentiles are devils: *but our Lord has formed the heavens above.

Glory and beauty belong to him; *holiness and grandeur decorate his sanctuary.

Bring to the Lord, ye kindred of the Gentiles, render to the Lord glory and honor. *Give that glory due to the name of the Lord.

Prepare sacrifices, and enter into his courts,

*adore the Lord in his holy sanctuary.

Let the earth be moved at his presence, *announce it to the nations: Behold the Lord reigneth.

For he hath established order on the earth, which shall not be disturbed. *The Lord will judge all people according to the truth of his holy law.

May the heavens rejoice, and may the earth, the sea, and all its fullness exult in transports of joy, *may the country around, and what it contains, be animated with gladness.

Then shall all the trees of the forests be revested with delight before the presence of the Lord, *because he cometh: for he is come to judge the earth.

He will judge the world with justice, *and all the people according to the truth of his holy law.

(Profound bow) Glory be to the Father, and to the Son, and to the Holy Ghost. *As it was in the beginning, is now, and ever shall be, world without end. Amen.

Anthem: Rejoice, O Virgin Mary, thou alone has rendered the Church triumphant over all the heresies spread through the earth.

Anthem

Cantor stands

Vouchsafe that I may praise thee, O sacred Virgin, obtain for me strength against thy enemies.

Psalm 97

Joy at the coming and reign of Christ

The Lord hath reigned, let the earth rejoice, *and may gladness be spread through many islands.

Clouds and darkness are around him, *justice and equity are the basis of his throne.

A flame of fire shall precede him, *and shall consume around all his enemies.

His lightnings flash throughout the world, *the earth saw the light and was moved to fear.

The mountains have melted away at the presence of the Lord, like wax before the fire; *the whole earth too has trembled at his presence.

The heavens have declared his righteousness, *and all the people have beheld his glory.

May they all be confounded who adore graven things, *and who glory in their idols.

Adore him, all ye his angels. *Sion hath heard his voice and was filled with gladness.

And the daughters of Judah have rejoiced, *on account of thy judgments, O Lord.

Because thou, O Lord, art most high above all the earth, *thou art exceedingly exalted above all gods.

All you who love the Lord, detest evil; *the Lord watcheth over the souls of his Saints and will deliver them from the power of sinners.

Light is risen for the just, *and joy for the upright of heart.

Ye just, rejoice in the Lord *and render glory to the author of all sanctity.

(Profound bow) Glory be to the Father, and to the Son, and to the Holy Ghost. *As it was in the beginning, is now, and ever shall be, world without end. Amen.

Anthem: Vouchsafe that I may praise thee, O sacred Virgin, obtain for me strength against thy enemies.

Anthem
Cantor stands

(Through the year) After thy child-birth thou didst remain an inviolate virgin, O Mother of God: make intercession for us.

(In Advent) The Angel of the Lord declared unto Mary, and she conceived by the Holy Ghost, *Alleluia.*

Psalm 98
Invitation to praise the Lord for the victories of Christ

Sing to the Lord a new canticle; *because he has wrought many wonderful things.

His strong hand has effected salvation, *and also his divine power.

The Lord hath made known the promised Savior, *he hath revealed his righteousness before the nations.

He hath been mindful of his mercy, *and of the inviolable promises he made Israel.

All the boundaries of the earth *have beheld the salvation which our God has wrought.

Let the whole earth praise God with joy, *may it chant forth, and rejoice, and sing canticles to him.

Sing praises to the Lord on the harp, with the melody of the psalter; *on the metal trumpet, accompanied with the music of the cornet.

Make joyful harmony before the Lord our king, *may the sea and all its fullness, may the earth and its inhabitants, be moved to exultation.

The rivers shall applaud, the mountains too shall rejoice before the Lord, *for he cometh to judge the earth.

He will judge the world with justice, *and all the people according to the truth of his holy law.

(Profound bow) Glory be to the Father, and to the Son, and to the Holy Ghost. *As it was in the beginning, is now, and ever shall be, world without end. Amen.

(Through the year) After thy child-birth thou didst remain an inviolate virgin, O Mother of God, make intercession for us.

(In Advent) The Angel of the Lord declared unto Mary, and she conceived by the Holy Ghost, *Alleluia.*

V. (Cantors) Grace is spread on thy lips.

R. (All) Therefore God hath blessed thee forever.

Stand

(V. (Presider) **Our Father,** (silently)...And lead us not into temptation

R. But deliver us from evil. Amen.

Absolution

V. (Presider) By the prayers and merits of the ever blessed Virgin Mary, and of all the saints, may the Lord bring us to the kingdom of heaven.

R. (All) Amen.

The reader bows the head toward the Presider and says:
(Reader) Pray, a blessing.

The Blessing
The reader remains bowing while the Presider says:

V. (Presider) May the Virgin Mary obtain for us the blessing of her divine Son.

R. (All) Amen.

Lessons
These following Lessons are recited throughout the year, except during Advent

The first Lesson
Sirach 24: 11-14
Sit

V. (Reader) I sought everywhere for a place of rest, and I shall dwell in the inheritance of the Lord. Then the Creator of the universe hath given me orders, and spoke unto me: He, who has created me, reposed in my tabernacle and said to me: Let thy dwelling be in Jacob, and thy inheritance in Israel, and take root among my elect. But thou, O Lord, have mercy on us.

R. (Cantors) Thanks be to God.

V. (Reader) O holy and immaculate Virginity, I know not with what praises to extol thy dignity

R. (All) Because whom the heavens could not contain, thou hast borne in thy womb.

V. (Reader) Blessed are thou among women, and blessed is the fruit of thy womb.

R. (All) Because whom the heavens could not contain, thou hast borne in thy womb.

The first Reader retires, and the second Reader goes to the lectern, according to the previous rubrics

(Reader) Pray, a blessing

The reader remains bowing while the Presider says:

V. May the Virgin of virgins make intercession for us to the Lord.

R. (All) Amen.

The Second Lesson
Ecclesiasticus 24:15-16
Douay Rheims 1899 American Edition (DRA)

V. (Reader) I have likewise dwelt in Sion, and have rested in the holy city, and my power was strengthened in Jerusalem. I settled myself among a people whom the Lord hath honored, and hath chosen for his portion and inheritance, and have fixed my abode in the company of all the saints. But thou, O Lord, have mercy on us.

R. (All) Thanks be to God.

V. (Reader) Blessed art thou, O Virgin Mary, who has borne the Lord and Creator of the world.

R. (All) Thou hast brought forth him who made thee, and remainest ever a virgin.

V. (Reader) Hail, Mary, full of grace, the Lord is with thee.

R. (All) Thou hast brought forth him who made thee, and remainest ever a virgin.

When the Te Deum is said after the third Lesson, the last verse of this Responsory is again repeated, thus:

V. (Reader: All bow profoundly) Glory be to the Father, and to the Son, and to the Holy Ghost.

R. (Choirs) Thou hast brought forth him who made thee, and remainest ever a virgin.

The Presider rises and turns to the one next in dignity, and with a profound bow of the head says:

(Reader) Pray, a blessing.

The one next in dignity says

V. May the Lord, through the intercession of the Virgin Mother, grant us salvation and peace.

R. (All) Amen.

All stand, while the Presider reads the Lesson from his/her place

The Third Lesson
Ecclesiasticus 24:17-20
Douay Rheims 1899 American Edition (DRA)

V. (Reader) I am exalted like the cedar on Lebanon, and as the cypress tree on Mount Sion: I have grown like the palm tree in Cades, and as the rose plant in Jericho: I have flourished like a fair olive tree in the fields, and as a plane tree watered by the stream. I yielded forth a fragrant smell like cinnamon and aromatic balm: and, like the best myrrh, I spread around the sweetest odor. But thou, O Lord, have mercy upon us.

R. (All) Thanks be to God.

The following Responsory is omitted when the Te Deum *is said.*

All sit

V. (Presider) Thou art truly happy, O sacred Virgin Mary, and most worthy of all praise.

R. (All) Because out of thee is risen the Sun of righteousness, Jesus Christ, our God.

V. (Presider) Pray for the people, intercede for the clergy, and plead for the devout female sex, let all be sensible of thine aid, who celebrate thy holy memory.

R. (All) Because of thee is risen the Sun of righteousness, Jesus Christ, our God.

V. (Presider, all bowing) Glory be to the Father, and to the Son, and to the Holy Ghost.

R. (All) Jesus Christ, our God.

Lessons In Advent

After the Psalms of the Nocturn, according to the order of the day, the following prayers and lessons are said:

Absolution
Stand

(Presider) By the prayers and merits of the ever blessed Virgin Mary, and of all the Saints, may the Lord bring us to the kingdom of heaven.

R. (All) Amen.

The reader bows the head to the Presider, saying:

V. (Reader) Pray, a blessing.

The reader remains bowing while the Presider says:

(Presider) May the Virgin Mary obtain for us the blessing of her divine Son.

R. (All) Amen.

The first Lesson
Luke 1:26-28
Sit

V. (Reader) The angel Gabriel was sent by God to a city of Galilee, called Nazareth, to a virgin espoused to a man, whose name was Joseph, of the house of David: and the virgin's name was Mary. And the angel having entered, said unto her: Hail, full of grace, the Lord is with thee: blessed art thou among women. But thou, O

Lord, have mercy on us.

R. (All) Thanks be to God.

V. (Reader) The angel Gabriel was sent to the Virgin Mary, espoused to Joseph, to announce to her the divine message; but the light of his countenance affrighted the sacred Virgin. Do not fear, Mary, thou hast found grace with the Lord:

R. (All) Behold, thou shalt conceive, and bring forth a Son, who shall be called the Son of the Most High.

V. (Reader) The Lord God shall give him the throne of his father David, and he shall eternally reign over the house of Jacob.

R. (All) Behold, thou shalt conceive, and bring forth a Son, who shall be called the Son of the Most High.

The first Reader retires, and the second Reader goes to the lectern, according to the previous rubrics

(Reader) Pray, a blessing.

V. (Presider) May the Virgin of virgins make intercession for us to the Lord.

R. (All) Amen.

The second Lesson
Luke 1:29-33

V. (Reader) Mary having heard these words, was much troubled, and reflected on what kind of salutation this could be. And the angel said to her: Do not fear, Mary, for thou hast found grace with God: behold, thou shalt conceive in thy womb, and shalt bring forth a Son, and shalt call his name Jesus. He shall be great and shall be called the Son of the Most High: the Lord God will give him the throne of his father David, and he shall eternally reign over the house of Jacob, and of his kingdom, there shall be no end. But thou, O Lord, have mercy on us.

R. (All) Thanks be to God.

V. (Reader) Hail, Mary, full of grace, the Lord is with thee. The Holy Ghost shall descend on thee, and the virtue of the Most High shall overshadow thee:

R. (Choirs) For the Holy One, who will be born of thee, shall be called the Son of God.

V. (Reader) How shall this be done, because I know not man? The angel answering, said to her:

R. (All) The Holy Ghost shall descend on thee, and the virtue of the Most High shall overshadow thee: For the Holy One, who will be born of thee, shall be called the Son of God.

The Presider rises and turns to the one next in dignity, and with a profound bow of the head says:

(Reader) Pray, a blessing.

The one next in dignity says:

V. (Presider) May the Lord, through the intercession of the Virgin Mother, grant us salvation and peace.

R. (All) Amen.

All stand, while the Presider reads the Lesson from his/her place

The third Lesson
Luke 1:34-38

V. (Presider) Then Mary said to the angel: How shall this be done, for I know not man? The angel answered her: The Holy Ghost shall descend on thee, and the virtue of the Most High shall overshadow thee: therefore the Holy One, who will be born of thee, shall be called the Son of God, and behold, thy cousin Elizabeth hath conceived a son in her old age; and this month is the sixth to her, who is called barren; for with God nothing shall be impossible. Mary then replied: Behold the handmaid of the Lord, be it done to me according to thy word. But thou, O Lord, have mercy on us.

R. (All) Thanks be to God.

V. (Presider) Receive, O Virgin Mary, the word which the Lord declared to thee by the ministry of the angel:

R. (All) Thou shalt conceive, and bring forth a Son, who will be both God and man: That thou mayest be called blessed among women.

V. (Presider) Thou shalt bring forth a son, and shalt suffer no detriment in thy virginity, thou shalt become a mother without ceasing to be a chaste virgin.

R. That thou mayest be called blessed among all women.

V. (Presider, all bowing) **Glory be to the Father, and to the Son, and to the Holy Ghost.**

R. That thou mayest be called blessed among all women.

On feasts of the Blessed Virgin Mary, the Te Deum may be said: then the last Responsory is omitted, the Glory Be is added to the second Responsory, and the last Versicle is again repeated.

Te Deum

The Te Deum may be sung:
* From the solemnity of Christmas to the Saturday before the ninth Sunday before Easter (Septuagesima Sunday)
* From the solemnity of Easter to the Saturday before the first Sunday of Advent.

When it is sung, the Responsory of the third Lesson is omitted, to the second Responsory the Glory Be to is added, and the last versicle repeated, as marked above.

This hymn is not sung
* In Advent,
* From the ninth Sunday before Easter (Septuagesima Sunday) to the Saturday after Easter

Notwithstanding, it may be sung on the following feasts of the Blessed Virgin Mary:
* The Conception on December 8th,
* The Expectation on December 18th,
* The Annunciation on March 25th,
* The Seven Dolors on Friday of Passion Week,
* Purification on February 2nd
when it falls on or after the ninth Sunday before Easter (Septuagesima Sunday)

Te Deum

(First Cantor and Choir) Thee sovereign God our grateful accents praise; *We own thee Lord, and bless thy wondrous ways.

To thee, eternal Father, earth's whole frame, *With loudest trumpets sounds immortal fame;

Lord, God of Hosts! For thee the heavenly powers, *With sounding antiphons fill the vaulted towers;

Thy Cherubim, thy Seraphim, thrice holy, cry, *To thee, O God, who dwells and reigns on high.

Both heaven and earth thy majesty display. *They owe their beauty to thy glorious ray.

Thy praises fill the loud apostles' choir. *The train of prophets in the song conspire.

Red hosts of martyrs in the chorus shine, *And vocal blood with vocal music join.

By these thy Church, inspired with heavenly art, *Around the world maintains a second part;

And tunes her sweetest notes, O God, for thee, *The Father of unbounded majesty,

The Son, adored co-partner of thy seat, *And equal everlasting Paraclete.

Thou King of Glory, Christ of the Most High *Thou co-eternal filial Deity;

Thou who to save the world's impending doom, *Vouchsafest to dwell within a virgin's womb

Old tyrant Death disarmed, before thee flew *The bolts of heaven and back the foldings drew,

To give access, and make the faithful way, *From God's right hand thy filial beams display.

Thou art to judge the living and the dead; *Then spare those souls for whom thy veins have bled.

(Genuflect)

O take us up amongst the blessed above, *To share with them in thy eternal love.

(Rise) Preserve, O Lord, thy people, and enhance, *Thy blessing on thy own inheritance.

Forever raise their hearts, and rule their ways; *Each day we bless thee, and proclaim thy praise.

No age shall fail to celebrate thy name, *Nor hour neglect thy everlasting fame.

Preserve our souls, O Lord, this day from ill: *Have mercy on us, Lord, have mercy still.

As we have hoped, do thou reward our pain: *We've hoped in thee, let not us hope in vain.

Lauds

Traditionally recited during the night as a nocturn, the laity may find it more convenient to recite in the morning before sunrise.

If Lauds is prayed by itself, and not together with Matins, the hour begins with the Hail Mary, prayed in silence. If Matins and Lauds are prayed together, the Hail Mary below is omitted)

Kneel

(Presider) **Hail Mary,** (silently) full of grace: the Lord is with thee. Blessed art thou amongst women, and blessed is the fruit of thy womb, Jesus. Holy Mary, Mother of God, pray for us sinners, now and at the hour of our death. Amen.

V. (Presider) Incline unto my aid, + O God.

R. O Lord, + make haste to help me.

(Profound bow) Glory be to the Father, and to the Son, and to the Holy Ghost. As it was in the beginning, is now, and ever shall be, world without end. Amen. *Alleluia.*

From Vespers on Saturday before the ninth Sunday before Easter (Septuagesima Sunday) till None on the Saturday after Easter, instead of Alleluia is said:

Praise be to thee, O Lord, king of eternal glory.

Anthem
The Cantor stands and recites the Anthem, etc.

(Throughout the year) Mary is taken up into heaven; the angels rejoice in her glory, and with praises bless the Lord.

(In Advent) The angel Gabriel was sent to the Virgin Mary, espoused to Joseph.

(Christmas time) O admirable intercourse! The creator of mankind, assuming a body animated with a soul, was pleased to be born of a virgin; and becoming man, without human concurrence, he made us partakers of his divine nature.

Psalm 93

The glory and stability of the Church of Christ

The Lord hath reigned, and is clothed with beauty, *he is covered with strength, and well girded.

(Sit) For he hath founded the earth on its basis, *which shall not be disturbed.

Thy throne was prepared before the world, *thou art from eternity.

The floods have risen, O Lord, *the floods have roared aloud.

The rivers have swelled their waves, *their roaring is the noise of many waters.

Wonderful are the surges of the sea, *but more wonderful is the Lord who rules over all things.

Thy testimonies are become exceedingly credible, *holiness becometh thy house, O Lord, unto length of days.

(Profound bow) Glory be to the Father, and to the Son, and to the Holy Ghost. *As it was in the beginning, is now, and ever shall be, world without end. Amen.

(Throughout the year) Mary is taken up into heaven; the angels rejoice in her glory, and with praises bless the Lord.

(In Advent) The angel Gabriel was sent to the Virgin Mary, espoused to Joseph.

(Christmas time) O admirable intercourse! the creator of mankind, assuming a body animated with a soul, was pleased to be born of a virgin; and becoming man, without human concurrence, he made us partakers of his divine nature.

Anthem

(Through the year) The Virgin Mary is taken up into the heavenly chamber, where the King of Kings sits on his throne, brilliant with stars.

(In Advent) Hail Mary, full of grace, the Lord is with thee: blessed art thou amongst women.

(Christmas time) When thou was born after an ineffable manner, the Scriptures were then fulfilled; thou didst descend like rain upon a fleece, to save mankind: O our God, we give thee praise.

Psalm 100

All are invited to praise the Lord

Sing joyfully to the Lord, ye people of the earth *serve the Lord with delight of heart.

Present yourselves before him *in transports of holy joy.

Know ye, that the Lord himself is the only God, *he hath made us, and not we ourselves.

We are his people, and the sheep of his pasture, *enter into the porches of his temple, singing his divine praises, and giving him glory.

Praise ye his name: for the Lord is sweet; his mercies are eternal, *and his truth endureth from generation to generation.

(Profound bow) Glory be to the Father, and to the Son, and to the Holy Ghost. *As it was in the beginning, is now, and ever shall be, world without end. Amen.

(Through the year) Antiphon: The Virgin Mary is taken up into the heavenly chamber, where the King of kings sits on his throne, brilliant with stars.

(In Advent) Antiphon: Hail Mary, full of grace, the Lord is with thee: blessed art thou amongst women.

(Christmas time) Antiphon: When thou wast born after an ineffable manner, the Scriptures were then fulfilled; thou didst descend like rain upon a fleece, to save mankind: O our God, we give thee praise.

Anthem

(Through the year) We run after the odor of thy perfumes: the young virgins have exceedingly loved thee.

(In Advent) Do not fear, Mary, thou hast found grace with the Lord; behold, thou shalt conceive and bring forth a Son.

(Christmas time) In the bush, which Moses saw burning without consuming, we acknowledge the preservation of thy admirable virginity: O mother of God, make intercession for us.

Psalm 63

A prayer in desolation and distress

O God, my God, *I watch unto thee from the dawn of the day.

My soul hath thirsted after thee; *oh, by how many titles doth my whole being belong to thee!

In this desert, uncultivated, and barren land, *I shall be in thy presence, if I were in the sanctuary, to contemplate thy power and thy glory.

For thy mercies are preferable to many lives, *my lips shall not cease to praise thee.

Thus I will bless thee all my life, *and I will lift up my hands to praise thy name.

May my soul be replenished with thy benedictions, as with the fatness of marrow, *and my mouth shall praise thee with rapturous joy.

I have called thee to mind on my bed at night, and in the morning I will meditate on thee, *because thou hast been my helper.

Under the cover of thy wings I will rejoice, *my soul is attached to thee: thy right hand hath protected me.

And my enemies have in vain sought my soul; they shall descend into the lower regions of the earth, *unto the justice of the sword they shall be delivered, and shall become a prey to ravenous foxes.

But the king shall rejoice in God: all, who swear by Him shall be glorified, *because he hath stopped the mouths of those who speak evil things.

The Gloria Patri *is not said here.*

Psalm 67
A prayer for the propagation of the Church

May God have mercy on us, and bless us, *may he regard us with a favorable countenance, and have mercy on us.

May we know Thy ways on earth, *and may all nations seek thy salvation.

May the people confess thee, O God, *may all present to thee their praises.

Let the nations be glad, and rejoice, *for thou dost judge the people with equity, and rulest over all the nations of the earth.

May the people confess thee, O God, *may all present to thee their praises: the earth hath yielded forth her fruit.

May the Lord, our God, bless us, may he give us his blessing, *and may all the bounds of the earth fear him.

(Profound bow) Glory be to the Father, and to the Son, and to the Holy Ghost. *As it was in the beginning, is now, and ever shall be, world without end. Amen.

(Through the year) We run after the odor of thy perfumes: the young virgins have exceedingly loved thee.

68

(In Advent) Do not fear, Mary, thou hast found grace with the Lord; behold, thou shalt conceive and bring forth a Son.

(Christmas time) In the bush, which Moses saw burning without consuming, we acknowledge the preservation of thy admirable virginity: O Mother of God, make intercession for us.

Anthem

(Through the year) Thou art blessed by the Lord, O daughter, for through thee we have been made partakers of the fruit of life.

(In Advent) The Lord will give him the throne of David, his father, and he shall reign forever.

(Christmas time) The root of Jesse hath budded forth: a star hath arisen out of Jacob: a virgin hath brought forth the Savior: we give thee praise, O our God.

Daniel 3

All ye works of the Lord, bless the Lord, *praise and extol him forever.

Bless the Lord, ye angels of the Lord, *ye heavens bless the Lord.

All ye waters, which lie suspended on the firmament, bless the Lord, *bless the Lord, all ye powers of the Lord.

Sun and moon, bless the Lord, *stars of the firmament, bless the Lord.

Every shower and dew, bless the Lord, *all ye tempestuous winds, bless the Lord.

Fire and heat, bless the Lord, *cold and heat, bless the Lord.

Dews and hoar-frosts, bless the Lord, *frost and cold, bless the Lord.

Ice and snow, bless the Lord, *nights and days, bless the Lord.

Light and darkness, bless the Lord, *lightnings and clouds, bless the Lord.

May the earth bless the Lord, *may it praise and extol him forever.

Mountains and hills, bless the Lord, *herbs and plants, bless the Lord.

Ye fountains, bless the Lord, *seas and rivers, bless the Lord.

Whales, and all ye creatures which live in the waters, bless the Lord, *all ye birds of the air, bless the Lord.

All beasts and cattle, bless the Lord, *ye children of men, bless the Lord.

May Israel bless the Lord; *may he praise and extol him forever.

Ye priests of the Lord, bless the Lord, *ye servants of the Lord, bless the Lord.

Spirits and souls of the just, bless the Lord, *ye holy and humble of heart, bless the Lord.

O Ananias, Azarias, Misael, bless ye the Lord, *praise and extol him forever.

Let us bless the Father, and the Son, with the Holy Ghost, *let us praise and glorify him forever.

Blessed art thou, O Lord, in the firmament of heaven, *to thee be rendered all praise, honor, and glory, forever.

The Gloria Patri is not said here

(Through the year): Thou art blessed by the Lord, O daughter, for through thee we have been made partakers of the fruit of life.

(In Advent): The Lord will give him the throne of David, his father, and he shall reign forever.

(Christmas time): The root of Jesse hath budded forth: a star hath arisen out of Jacob: a virgin hath brought forth the Savior: we give thee praise, O our God.

Anthem

(Through the year): Thou art fair and beautiful, O daughter of Jerusalem, formidable as an army in battle array.

(In Advent): Behold the handmaid of the Lord, be it done unto me according to thy word.

(Christmas time): Behold Mary hath borne to us the Savior, whom John seeing, cried out: Behold the Lamb of God, behold him, who taketh away the sins of the world, *Alleluia.*

Psalm 148

All creatures invited to praise God

Praise the Lord in the heavens, *praise him in the highest places.

Praise him, all ye his angels, *praise him, ye celestial powers.

Praise him, sun and moon, *praise him, all ye stars and light.

Praise him, O heaven of heavens, *and may the waters that are over the firmament praise the name of the Lord.

For he hath spoken the word, and all things were made, *he hath commanded, and they were created.

He hath established his works for length of ages, *he

prescribed to them his wise regulations, which shall not be transgressed.

Praise the Lord, from the earth, *ye dragons and all ye depths.

Fire, hail, snow, ice, and stormy winds *which obey his orders.

Mountains and all hills, *fruit-bearing trees, and all cedars.

Beasts, and herds of cattle, *reptiles and birds of the air.

Kings of the earth, and all ye people, *princes, and judges of the earth.

Young men and maidens: the old with the young, let them praise the name of the Lord, *for his name alone is most worthy of all praise.

His praise is above heaven and earth, *and he hath exalted the power of his people.

May hymns of praise be rendered to him by all his saints, *by the children of Israel, his cherished people.

The Gloria Patri is not said here

Psalm 149
The Church is particularly bound to praise God

Sing to the Lord a new canticle, *may his praises resound in the assembly of the Saints.

May Israel rejoice in the God, who made him, *may the sons of Sion exult in their king.

May they celebrate his name in choir, *and honor him by concert on the timbrel and the psaltery.

For the Lord is well pleased with his people, *and he will exalt the meek unto salvation.

The Saints in glory shall be filled with joy, *they shall rejoice on their couches.

Sublime praises of God are in their mouths, *and two-edged swords in their hands,

To execute vengeance on the nations, *and chastisement on the people;

To bind their kings in fetters, *and their nobles with iron manacles.

They shall thus exercise the decreed justice, *this glory is reserved for all his saints.

The Gloria Patri is not said here

Psalm 150
An exhortation to praise God

Praise the Lord in his sanctuary, *praise him in the firmament of his power.

Praise him in his mighty deeds, *praise him according to his exceeding greatness.

Praise him with the sound of the trumpet, *praise him on the psaltery and the harp.

Praise him on the timbrel and in choir, *praise him on stringed instruments, and on the organ.

Praise him with the best sounding cymbals, praise him on instruments of jubilee, *may every living creature praise the Lord.

(Profound bow) Glory be to the Father, and to the Son, and to the Holy Ghost. *As it was in the beginning, is now, and ever shall be, world without end. Amen.

(Through the year): Thou art fair and beautiful, O daughter of Jerusalem, formidable as an army in battle array.

(In Advent): Behold the handmaid of the Lord, be it done unto me according to thy word.

(Christmas time): Behold Mary hath borne to us the Savior, whom John seeing cried out: Behold the Lamb of God, behold him, who taketh away the sins of the world, alleluia.

The Little Chapter through the year except in Advent
Song of Songs 6: 9
Stand

(Presider) The daughters of Sion beheld her, and declared her most blessed, and queens have highly praised her.

R. (All) Thanks be to God.

The Little Chapter in Advent
Isaiah 11: 1
Stand

(Presider) There shall spring forth a branch out of the root of Jesse, and a flower shall arise out of its stock; and the Spirit of the Lord shall rest upon him.

R. (All) Thanks be to God.

The first Cantor begins the hymn, and his Choir continues it; the second strophe is said by the opposite Choir. At the last strophe, both Choirs combine, and bow profoundly

O Mary! Whilst Thy Maker Blest

O Gloriosa Virginum

V. (Cantor) Blessed art thou among women.
R. (All) And blessed is the fruit of thy womb.

O Gloriosa Virginum

São Pedro Partituras - 2017
saopedropartituras.blogspot.com

With permission of the copyright holder
https://www.youtube.com/watch?v=rjajAe6jtkQ

V. (Cantor) Blessed art thou among women.
R. (All) And blessed is the fruit of thy womb.

Lauds

Anthem

The Cantor begins the Anthem

(Through the year): O blessed Mary, Mother of God, and ever virgin, temple of the Lord, and sanctuary of the Holy Ghost, thou alone didst please our Lord Jesus Christ, in a most singular and perfect manner: pray for the people, plead for the clergy, and intercede for the devout female sex.

(In Easter time): O Queen of heaven, rejoice, *Alleluia*, because He, whom thou didst deserve to bear, alleluia, is risen again, as He foretold, alleluia: pray for us to God, alleluia.

(In Advent): The Holy Ghost shall come upon thee, Mary: do not fear, thou shalt have in thy womb the Son of God, alleluia.

(Christmas time): A most sublime mystery is made manifest on this day: wonders are wrought in nature; God is made man, still remaining what he was; he assumed what he was not; he suffered no mixture, nor division.

The Canticle of Zachariah. Luke 1: 68-79

Stand

(Cantor) + Blessed be the Lord, the God of Israel, *because he hath visited and effected the redemption of his people.

And hath raised up a powerful Savior for us, *in the house of David, his servant.

As he promised by the mouth of his holy prophets, *from the beginning,

To save us from our enemies, *and from the hands of all who hate us.

To communicate his mercy to us, as well as to our fathers, *and to recall to mind the holy covenant made to them.

The oath, which he hath sworn to our father Abraham, *that he would grant us the grace.

That, being rescued from the fear and power of our enemies, we may serve him in holiness and righteousness in his presence, *all the days of our lives.

And thou, O happy child, shalt be called the prophet of the Most High, *for thou shalt go before the face of the Lord to prepare his ways, To give his people the knowledge of salvation *unto the remission of their sins.

Through the bowels of the mercy of our God, *with which he, like the rising sun from on high, hath visited us.

To give light to those, who sit in darkness and in the shade of death, *to guide our feet into the ways of peace.

(Profound bow) Glory be to the Father, and to the Son, and to the Holy Ghost. *As it was in the beginning, is now, and ever shall be, world without end. Amen.

(Through the year): O blessed Mary, Mother of God, and ever virgin, temple of the Lord, and sanctuary of the Holy Ghost, thou alone didst please our Lord Jesus Christ, in a most singular and perfect manner: pray for the people, plead for the clergy, and intercede for the devout female sex.

(In Easter time): O Queen of heaven, rejoice, *Alleluia*, because He, whom thou didst deserve to bear, alleluia, is risen again, as He foretold, alleluia: pray for us to God, alleluia.

(In Advent): The Holy Ghost shall come upon thee, Mary: do not fear, thou shalt have in thy womb the Son of God, alleluia.

(Christmas time): A most sublime mystery is made manifest on this day: wonders are wrought in nature; God is made man, still remaining what he was; he assumed what he was not; he suffered no mixture, nor division.

(First Choir) Lord, have mercy on us,

(Second Choir) Christ, have mercy on us,

(All) Lord, have mercy on us.

V. (Presider) O Lord, hear my prayer.

R. (All) And let my cry come unto thee.

Let us pray

The prayer through the year, except at Christmas time
All bow

(Presider) O God, who was pleased that thy eternal Word, when the angel delivered his message, should take flesh in the womb of the blessed Virgin Mary, give ear to our humble petitions, and grant that we, who believe her to be truly the Mother of God, may be assisted by her prayers, through the same Christ our Lord. (Rise)

R. (All) Amen.

At Christmas time
All bow

(Presider) O God, who, by the fruitful virginity of blessed Mary, has given to mankind the rewards of eternal salvation, grant, we beseech thee, that we may experience her intercession for us, by whom we deserved to receive the author of life, our Lord Jesus Christ thy Son.

(Rise) R. (All) Amen.

Commemoration of the Saints
through the year, except in Advent

Anthem

(All) All ye saints of God, vouchsafe to make intercession for the salvation of us, and of all mankind.

V. (Cantors) Rejoice in the Lord, ye just, and be exceedingly glad.

R. (All) And exult in glory, all ye upright of heart.

Let us pray

(Presider) Protect, O Lord, thy people, and grant us thy continual assistance, which we humbly beg with confidence, through the intercession of St. Peter and St. Paul, and of thy other apostles. May all the saints, we beseech thee, O Lord, always assist our weakness, that whilst we celebrate their merits we may experience their protection; grant us thy peace in our days, and banish all evils from thy Church: prosperously guide the steps, actions, and desires of us, and of all thy servants, in the way of salvation: give eternal blessings to our benefactors, and grant everlasting rest to all the faithful departed. Through our Lord Jesus Christ, thy son, who liveth and reigneth with thee and the Holy Ghost, one God, world without end.

R. (All) Amen.

Then is recited one of the Anthems of the Blessed Virgin Mary

Commemoration of the Saints in Advent

Anthem

(All) Behold, the Lord will come, and all his saints with him: and there shall be a great light on that day, alleluia.

V. (Cantors) Behold, the Lord shall appear on a bright cloud.

R. (All) And with him thousands of saints.

Let us pray

(Presider) Visit and purify our consciences, O God, that Jesus Christ, thy Son, our Lord, coming with all his Saints, may find in us an abode prepared for his reception: who liveth and reigneth with thee and the Holy Ghost, one God, world without end.
R. Amen.

V. (Cantors) O Lord, hear my prayer.
R. (All) And let my cry come unto thee.
V. (Cantors) Let us bless the Lord.
R. (All) Thanks be to God.
V. (Presider) May the souls of the faithful departed, through the mercy of God, rest in peace.
R. (All) Amen.
V. (Presider) **Our Father** *in silence*...And lead us not into temptation
R. But deliver us from evil.
V. (Cantors) May the Lord grant us his peace.
R. (All) And life everlasting. Amen.

The Presider prays the Prayer after the Office, and the Choirs respond

Prime

Recited at 6 a.m.

Kneel

(Silently) *O divine and adorable Lord Jesus Christ, who hast graciously redeemed us by thy bitter passion and death, we offer up this hour of Prime to thy honor and glory, and most humbly beseech thee, through the great humility thou didst undergo, in being convicted before the false tribunals of Pilate and Herod, where thou wast reviled by the soldiery, clothed like a fool, and degraded below the worst of criminals, to grant us true humility of heart, and sincere sentiments of our own wretchedness, misery, poverty, blindness, and destitution, that we may never esteem ourselves above the lowest of our fellow-creatures, but always acknowledge ourselves truly the worst of sinners, so that our extreme misery may excite thy tender compassion and infinite goodness to forgive us all our sins, to replenish us with thy divine grace here, and to elevate us to eternal glory in heaven. Amen.*

Stand

+ **Hail, Mary**, full of grace, the Lord is with thee. Blessed art thou amongst women, and blessed is the fruit of thy womb, Jesus. Holy Mary, Mother of God, pray for us sinners, now, and in the hour of our death. Amen.

V. (Presider) Incline unto my aid, + O God.

R. (All) O Lord, + make haste to help me.

(Profound bow) Glory be to the Father, and to the Son, and to the Holy Ghost. *As it was in the beginning, is now, and ever shall be, world without end. Amen, *Alleluia.*

From Vespers on Saturday before the ninth Sunday before Easter (Septuagesima Sunday) till None on the Saturday after Easter, instead of Alleluia is said:

Praise be to thee, O Lord, king of eternal glory.

The first Cantor begins the hymn, and his Choir continues it; the second strophe is said by the opposite Choir, and so on. At the last strophe, both Choirs combine, and bow profoundly

Remember Thou Creator Lord

Memento, rerum Conditor

Re - mem - ber thou, Cre -
O Hap - py Ma - ry
To thee, O Je - sus

a - tor Lord, the Fath - er God's co -
full of grace, dear Mo - ther of the
Ma - ry's Son, be e - ver - las - ting

e - qual Word, to save man - kind, from
Prince - of Peace, pro - tect us from our
ho - mage done, to God the Fath - er

vir - gin's womb, our hu - man na - ture
e - vil foe, and bliss at death on
we re - peat the same, and to the

didst as - sume. A - men
us bes - tow.
Pa - ra clete.

Memento Rerum Conditor

1

Me- men - to, re - rum Con - di - tor, nos-
Ma - ri - a Ma - ter gra - ti - ae, Dul-
Je - su ti - bi sit glo - ri - a, qui

tri quod o - lim cor - -po-ris, Sa- cra - ta_ab al - vo
cis Pa- rens cle- men - -ti-ae, tu nos ab hos - te
na - tus es de Vir - -gi-ne, Cum Pa - tre_et al - mo

Vir - gi-nis, Nas- cen - do, for- mam sum - -pse-ris
pro - te - ge, Et mor - tis ho - ra sus - -ci - pe
Spi - ri - tu In sem - pi-ter - na sae - -cu - la

A - men

Anthem

The first Cantor stands and recites the Anthem

(Through the year). Mary is taken up into heaven: the angels rejoice, and with praises bless the Lord.

(In Advent). The angel Gabriel was sent to the Virgin Mary, espoused to Joseph.

(Christmas time). O admirable intercourse! The Creator of mankind, assuming a body animated with a soul, was pleased to be born of a virgin, and becoming man without human concurrence, made us partakers of his divine nature.

Psalm 54

Stand

A prayer for help in distress

Save me, O God, in thy name, *and in thy power do me justice.

(Sit) O God, graciously hear my prayer, *give ear to my words.

For strangers have risen up against me, and the strong ones have sought to take away my soul, *and they have not been mindful of the presence of God.

For behold, God is my helper, *and the Lord is the protector of my soul.

Turn back on my enemies the evils which they wish to do to me, *and destroy them according to the truth of thy words.

I will freely sacrifice to thee *and will praise thy holy name, O Lord: because it is just.

For thou hast rescued me from all trouble, *and I have regarded my enemies without fear.

(Profound bow) Glory be to the Father, and to the Son, and to the Holy Ghost. *As it was in the beginning, is now, and ever shall be, world without end. Amen, *Alleluia.*

Psalm 85

Prayer to obtain the complete restoration of Israel

O Lord, thou hast blessed thy land, *thou hast set free the captives of Jacob.

Thou hast forgiven the iniquity of thy people, *thou hast pardoned all their sins.

Thou hast mitigated all thine anger, *and withdrawn from us thy indignation.

Convert us to thee, O God, our Savior, *and turn away thy wrath from us.

Wilt thou be forever angry with us? *Or wilt thou continue thy wrath from generation to generation?

O God, thou wilt cheer us with thy reconciliation, *and thy people shall rejoice in thee.

Show us, O Lord, thy mercy, *and grant us thy salvation.

I will hear what the Lord God will speak to me, *for he will speak peace unto his people.

He will announce it to his Saints, *and to those whose heart is truly converted to him.

Surely his salvation is near to those who fear him, *that his glory may dwell among us.

Mercy and truth have met each other, *justice and peace have kissed.

Truth is sprung out of the earth, *and justice hath regarded us from the height of heaven.

For the Lord will communicate his goodness, *and the earth shall yield her fruit.

Justice shall proceed before him, *and shall direct his steps in the true path.

(Profound bow) Glory be to the Father, and to the Son, and to the Holy Ghost. *As it was in the beginning, is now, and ever shall be, world without end. Amen, *Alleluia.*

Psalm 117
Exhortation to praise God
Praise the Lord, all ye nations, *praise him, all ye people.

For his mercy is confirmed upon us, *and the truth of the Lord remaineth forever.

(Profound bow) Glory be to the Father, and to the Son, and to the Holy Ghost. *As it was in the beginning, is now, and ever shall be, world without end. Amen, *Alleluia.*

(Through the year). Mary is taken up into heaven: the angels rejoice, and with praises bless the Lord.

(In Advent). The angel Gabriel was sent to the Virgin Mary, espoused to Joseph.

(Christmas time). O admirable intercourse! The Creator of mankind, assuming a body animated with a soul, was pleased to be born of a virgin, and becoming man without human concurrence, made us partakers of his divine nature.

The Little Chapter through the year, except in Advent

Song of Songs 6: 10
V. (Presider) Who is she, that cometh forth as the morning rising, beautiful like the moon, bright as the sun, formidable as an army in battle array?

R. (All) Thanks be to God.

The Little Chapter in Advent

Isaiah 7:14-15

V. (Presider) Behold, a virgin shall conceive, and bring forth a son, and his name shall be called Emmanuel. He shall eat butter and honey, that he may know how to reject evil, and choose good.

R. (All) Thanks be to God.

V. (Cantors) Vouchsafe, O sacred Virgin, to accept my praises.

R. (All) Give me strength against thy enemies.

(First Choir) Lord, have mercy on us.

(Second Choir) Christ, have mercy on us.

(All) Lord, have mercy on us.

V. (Cantors) O Lord, hear my prayer.

R. (All) And let my cry come unto thee.

Let us pray
Presider

(Through the year) O God, who was pleased to make choice of the chaste womb of the blessed Virgin Mary for thy abode; grant, we beseech thee, that, being protected by the assistance of her intercession, we may celebrate her memory with spiritual joy: Who livest and reignest with the Father and the Holy Ghost, one God, world without end.

R. (All) Amen.

(In Advent) O God, who was pleased that thy eternal Word, when the angel delivered his message, should take flesh in the womb of the blessed Virgin Mary, give ear to our humble petitions, and grant that we, who believe her to be truly the mother of God, may be assisted by her prayers. Through the same Lord Jesus Christ thy Son, who liveth and reigneth with thee and the Holy Ghost, one God, world without end.

R. (All) Amen.

(Christmas time) O God, who, by the fruitful virginity of blessed Mary, has given to mankind the rewards of eternal salvation, grant, we beseech thee, that we may experience her intercession, by whom we have received the author of life, our Lord Jesus Christ, thy Son: Who liveth and reigneth with thee and the Holy Ghost, one God, world without end.

R. (All) Amen.

V. (Cantors) O Lord, hear my prayer.
R. (All) And let my cry come unto thee.
V. (Cantors) Let us bless the Lord.
R. (All) Thanks be to God.
V. (Presider) May the souls of the faithful departed, through the mercy of God, rest in peace.
R. (All) Amen.

The Presider prays the Prayer after the Office, and the Choirs respond

The Hours of Our Lady

Terce

Kneel

(Silently) *O divine and adorable Lord, Jesus Christ, who has graciously redeemed us by thy bitter passion and death, we offer up this hour of Terce to thy honor and glory: and most humbly beseech thee, through the torments thou didst endure in being cruelly scourged at a pillar, crowned with thorns, and unjustly condemned to be crucified, to grant us patience and longanimity under the scourges of temporal afflictions, courage to walk in the thorny road to the narrow gate, which opens to bliss, and perseverance under all the crosses of this life, which are the portion of the elect, that by suffering for our sins we may fully satisfy thy divine justice on earth, and may enter into thy glory immediately after death. Amen.*

Stand

+ **Hail Mary**, full of grace, the Lord is with thee. Blessed art thou among women, and blessed is the fruit of thy womb, Jesus. Holy Mary, Mother of God, pray for us sinners, now, and in the hour of our death. Amen.

V. (Presider) Incline unto my aid, + O God.

R. O Lord, + make haste to help me.

(Profound bow) Glory be to the Father, and to the Son, and to the Holy Ghost. *As it was in the beginning, is now, and ever shall be, world without end. Amen, *Alleluia*.

From Vespers on Saturday before the ninth Sunday before Easter (Septuagesima Sunday till None on the Saturday after Easter, instead of Alleluia is said:

Praise be to thee, O Lord, king of eternal glory.

The first Cantor begins the hymn, and his Choir continues it; the second strophe is said by the opposite Choir, and so on. At the last strophe, both Choirs combine, and bow profoundly

Remember Thou Creator Lord

Memento, rerum Conditor

Re - mem - ber thou, Cre - a - tor Lord, the Fath - er God's co - e - qual Word, to save man - kind, from vir - gin's womb, our didst as - sume.
O Hap - py Ma - ry full of grace, dear Mo - ther of the Prince - of Peace, pro - tect us from our e - vil foe, and bliss at death us bes - tow.
To thee, O Je - sus Ma - ry's Son, be e - ver - las - ting ho - mage done, to God the Fath - er we re - peat the same, and to the Pa - ra clete.

A - men

Memento Rerum Conditor

Me- men - to, re - rum Con - di - tor, nos-
Ma- ri - a Ma- ter gra - ti - ae, Dul-
Je - su ti - bi sit glo - ri - a, qui

tri quod o - lim cor - -po-ris, Sa- cra - ta_ab al - vo
cis Pa- rens cle- men - -ti-ae, tu nos ab hos - te
na - tus es de Vir - -gi- ne, Cum Pa- tre_et al - mo

Vir - gi - nis, Nas - cen - do, for - mam sum - -pse - ris
pro - te - ge, Et mor - tis ho - ra sus - - ci - pe
Spi - ri - tu In sem - pi - ter - na sae - - cu - la

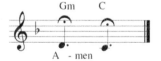

A - men

Anthem

The first Cantor stands and recites the Anthem, etc.

(Through the year) The Virgin Mary is taken up into the heavenly chamber where the King of kings sits on his starry throne.

(In Advent) Ant. Hail, Mary, full of grace, the Lord is with thee; blessed art thou among women.

(Christmas time) When thou was born after an ineffable manner, the Scriptures were then fulfilled: thou didst descend like rain upon a fleece, to save mankind: O our God, we give thee praise.

Psalm 120

Stand

A prayer against perfidious enemies

I cried out to the Lord in my extreme distress, *and he graciously heard me.

(Sit) O Lord, deliver my soul from unjust lips *and from a deceitful tongue.

What shall be done to thee, or what punishment shalt thou receive, *for thy deceitful tongue?

Thou shalt feel the sharp arrows of the mighty, *accompanied with destructive burning coals.

How miserable I am, that my exile is so prolonged! I dwell here among the inhabitants of Cedar, *my soul hath been long a sojourner.

I was peaceable with those who hated peace, *when I spoke to them, they opposed me without any cause.

(Profound bow) Glory be to the Father, and to the Son, and to the Holy Ghost. *As it was in the beginning, is now, and ever shall be, world without end. Amen, *Alleluia.*

Psalm 121

God is keeper of His servants

I lifted up my eyes toward the mountains, *from whence I expect assistance.

My help is from the Lord, *who made heaven and earth.

May he not suffer thy foot to be moved, *neither may he slumber, who is thy guardian.

Behold, he shall neither slumber nor sleep, *that keepeth Israel.

The Lord watcheth over thee, the Lord is thy protector, *he is at thy right hand.

The sun shall not burn thee by day, *nor shall the moon molest thee by night.

The Lord preserveth thee from all evil, *may the Lord still protect thy soul.

May the Lord watch over thee coming in and going out, *now and forevermore.

(Profound bow) Glory be to the Father, and to the Son, and to the Holy Ghost. *As it was in the beginning, is now, and ever shall be, world without end. Amen, *Alleluia.*

Psalm 122

Joy of the pilgrim entering Jerusalem

I rejoiced in what hath been told me, *we are to go up to the house of the Lord.

Our feet have stood *in thy courts, O Jerusalem.

Jerusalem, which is now building like a city, *all whose parts are well combined.

For thither the tribes went up, the tribes of the Lord, *according to the ordinances given to Israel, to praise the name of the Lord.

For there were placed the judgment-seats, *the judgment-seats over the house of David.

Pray for whatever maketh for the peace of Jerusalem, *and may plenty be to all who love thee.

May peace be in thy strength, *and plenty within thy walls.

For the sake of my brethren and of all my neighbors, *I have advocated thy peace.

For the sake of the house of the Lord our God, *I have sought good things for thee.

(Profound bow) Glory be to the Father, and to the Son, and to the Holy Ghost. *As it was in the beginning, is now, and ever shall be, world without end. Amen, *Alleluia.*

(Through the year) The Virgin Mary is taken up into the heavenly chamber where the King of kings sits on his starry throne.

(In Advent) Ant. Hail, Mary, full of grace, the Lord is with thee; blessed art thou among women.

(Christmas time) When thou was born after an ineffable manner, the Scriptures were then fulfilled: thou didst descend like rain upon a fleece, to save mankind: O our God, we give thee praise.

Little Chapter through the year,
except in Advent

Sirach 24:15
Douay Rheims 1899 American Version

V. (Presider) And so was I established in Sion, and in the holy city likewise I rested, and my power was in Jerusalem.

R. Thanks be to God.

The Little Chapter in Advent

Isaiah 11:1-2

There shall spring forth a branch out of the root of Jesse, and a flower shall arise out of its stock: and the Spirit of the Lord shall rest upon Him.

R. Thanks be to God.

V. Grace is spread on thy lips.

R. Therefore God hath blessed thee forever.

(First Choir) Lord, have mercy on us.

(Second Choir) Christ, have mercy on us.

(All) Lord, have mercy on us.

V. (Cantors) O Lord, hear my prayer.

R. (All) And let my cry come unto thee.

The Prayer through the year,
except in Advent

O God, who by the fruitful virginity of blessed Mary, has given to mankind the rewards of eternal salvation; grant, we beseech thee, that we may experience her intercession for us, by whom we deserved to receive the author of life, our Lord Jesus Christ thy Son, who liveth and reigneth with thee and the Holy Ghost, one God, world without end. Amen.

Let us pray.

In Advent

O God, who was pleased that thy eternal Word, when the angel delivered his message, should take flesh in the womb of the blessed Virgin Mary; give ear to our humble petitions, and grant

92

that we, who believe her to be truly the Mother of God, may be helped by her prayers. Through the same Lord, Jesus Christ, who liveth and reigneth with thee and the Holy Ghost, one God, world without end. Amen.

V. (Cantors) O Lord, hear my prayer.

R. (All) And let my cry come unto thee.

V. (Cantors) Let us bless the Lord.

R. (All) Thanks be to God.

V. (Presider) May the souls of the faithful departed, through the mercy of God, rest in peace.

R. (All) Amen.

The Presider prays the Prayer after the Office, and the Choirs respond

The Hours of Our Lady

Sext

Recited at noon

Kneel

*(Silently) O divine and adorable Lord, Jesus Christ, who has graciously
redeemed us by thy bitter passion and death, we offer up this hour of Sext to
thy honor and glory; and most humbly beseech thee, through the fainting thou
didst experience in bearing the cross from Pilate's tribunal to Calvary, and
the excessive pains thou didst suffer when thy tender hands and feet were
cruelly pierced through with gross nails, and fastened to the cross, to grant us
thy strengthening grace to arise immediately whenever we fall into sin, and to
restrain our hands, our feet, and our other sensitive powers from injuring our
neighbor, and from evil deeds, that we may rise up, and go to our celestial
Father with our hands replete with good works, to merit thy eternal rewards.
Amen.*

Stand

+ **Hail, Mary,** full of grace, the Lord is with thee. Blessed art
thou among women, and blessed is the fruit of thy womb, Jesus.
Holy Mary, Mother of God, pray for us sinners, now, and in the
hour of our death. Amen.

V. (Presider) Incline unto my aid, + O God.

R. O Lord, + make haste to help me.

(Profound bow) Glory be to the Father, and to the Son, and to the
Holy Ghost. As it was in the beginning, is now, and ever shall be,
world without end. Amen, *Alleluia.*

*From Vespers on Saturday before the ninth Sunday before
Easter (Septuagesima Sunday) till None on the Saturday
after Easter, instead of Alleluia is said:*

Praise be to thee, O Lord, king of eternal glory.

*The first Cantor begins the hymn, and his Choir continues
it; the second strophe is said by the opposite Choir, and so
on. At the last strophe, both Choirs combine, and bow
profoundly*

Remember Thou Creator Lord

Memento, rerum Conditor

1

São Pedro Partituras - 2017
saopedropartituras.blogspot.com

With permission of the copyright holder
https://www.youtube.com/watch?v=wFZONAPUtAY

Memento Rerum Conditor

F   Dm   B♭   C   F   C⁷

Me- men - to, re - rum Con - di- tor, nos-
Ma- ri - a Ma - ter gra - ti- ae, Dul-
Je- su ti - bi sit glo - ri - a, qui

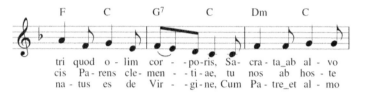

F   C   G⁷   C   Dm   C

tri quod o - lim cor - -po-ris, Sa- cra - ta_ab al - vo
cis Pa - rens cle- men - -ti- ae, tu nos ab hos - te
na - tus es de Vir - -gi- ne, Cum Pa - tre_et al - mo

Gm   C   Am   Dm   B♭   C

Vir - gi- nis, Nas - cen - do, for - mam sum - -pse - ris
pro - te - ge, Et mor - tis ho - ra sus - - ci - pe
Spi - ri - tu In sem - pi- ter - na sae - -cu - la

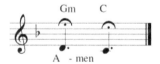

Gm   C

A - men

Anthem

If prayed in a Church, the Cantors rise and genuflect to the altar, go to the lectern, salute their Choirs, and the first Cantor recites the Anthem standing

(Through the year) We run after the odor of thy perfumes: the young virgins have exceedingly loved thee.

(In Advent) Fear not, Mary, thou hast found grace with the Lord: behold, thou shalt conceive, and bring forth a son.

(Christmas time) In the bush, which Moses saw burn without consuming, we acknowledge the preservation of thy admirable virginity: O Mother of God, make intercession for us.

Psalm 123

Stand

A prayer in affliction

To thee have I lifted up my eyes, *who dwellest in heaven.

(Sit) Behold, as the eyes of servants *look to the bountiful hands of their masters.

And as the eyes of the handmaid look to the bountiful hands of her mistress, *so are our eyes fixed on the Lord, our God, until he have mercy upon us.

Have mercy on us, O Lord, have mercy on us; *for we are overwhelmed with humiliation.

For our soul is deeply afflicted, *being an object of reproach to the rich, and of contempt to the proud.

(Profound bow) Glory be to the Father, and to the Son, and to the Holy Ghost. *As it was in the beginning, is now, and ever shall be, world without end. Amen, *Alleluia.*

Psalm 124

The Church gives glory to God for her deliverance from her enemies

If it had not been that the Lord was with us, let Israel now say, *If it had not been that the Lord was with us,

When men rose up against us, *perhaps they had engulfed us alive:

When their fury raged against us, *they would have probably overpowered us, like a raging wave, and sunk us.

Our soul has waded across the torrent, *perhaps our soul has passed through waves of the most intolerable evils.

Blessed be the Lord, *who has not delivered us a prey to be torn by their teeth.

Our soul has been saved, *like a sparrow which escapes the snare of the fowlers.

The snare has been broken, *and we are delivered.

Our help is in the name of the Lord, *who made heaven and earth.

(Profound bow) Glory be to the Father, and to the Son, and to the Holy Ghost. *As it was in the beginning, is now, and ever shall be, world without end. Amen, *Alleluia.*

Psalm 125
God protects the just who have confidence in Him

They who trust in the Lord shall be as mount Sion, *he who dwelleth in Jerusalem shall never be disturbed.

Mountains encompass it on every side, *the Lord doth protect his people, now, and forevermore.

Because the Lord will not permit the chastisement of sinners to fall on the righteous, *lest the just are induced to stain their hands with iniquity.

Be kind, O Lord, to those who are good, *and to the upright of heart.

But such as are inclined to deceive and to ensnare; the Lord shall number among the workers of iniquity: *peace upon Israel.

(Profound bow) Glory be to the Father, and to the Son, and to the Holy Ghost. *As it was in the beginning, is now, and ever shall be, world without end. Amen, *Alleluia.*

(Through the year) We run after the odor of thy perfumes: the young virgins have exceedingly loved thee.

(In Advent) Fear not, Mary, thou hast found grace with the Lord: behold, thou shalt conceive, and bring forth a son.

(Christmas time) In the bush, which Moses saw burn without consuming, we acknowledge the preservation of thy admirable virginity: O Mother of God, make intercession for us.

Little Chapter through the year, except in Advent

Sirach 24:16
Douay Rheims 1899 American Version

V. (Presider) I settled myself among a people whom the Lord hath honored, and hath chosen for his portion and inheritance, and I have fixed my abode in the company of all the Saints

R. (All) Thanks be to God.

The Little Chapter In Advent

Luke 1:32-33

V. (Presider) The Lord God will give him the throne of his Father David, and he will eternally reign over the house of Jacob, and his kingdom shall never end.

R. (All) Thanks be to God.

V. (Presider) Blessed art thou among women.

R. (All) And blessed is the fruit of thy womb.

(First Choir) Lord, have mercy on us.

(Second Choir) Christ, have mercy on us.

(All) Lord, have mercy on us.

V. (Cantors) O Lord, hear my prayer.

R. (All) And let my cry come unto thee.

Let us pray
Presider

(Through the year) Grant us, O merciful God, strength against all weakness; that we, who celebrate the memory of the holy Mother of God, may by the help of her intercession rise again from our iniquities. Through the same Lord Jesus Christ thy Son, who liveth and reigneth with thee and the Holy Ghost, one God, world without end.

R. Amen.

(In Advent) O God, who was pleased that thy eternal Word, when the angel delivered his message, should take flesh in the womb of the blessed Virgin Mary, give ear to our humble petitions, and grant, that we who believe her to be truly the mother of God, may be helped by her prayers. Through the same Lord Jesus Christ, thy Son, who liveth and reigneth with thee and the Holy Ghost, one God, world without end.

R. Amen.

(Christmas time) O God, who, by the fruitful virginity of blessed Mary, has given to mankind the rewards of eternal salvation: grant, we beseech thee, that we may experience her intercession for us, by whom we deserved to receive the Author of life, our Lord Jesus

Christ, thy Son, who liveth and reigneth with thee and the Holy Ghost, one God, world without end.

R. Amen.

V. (Cantors) O Lord, hear my prayer.

R. (All) And let my cry come unto thee.

V. (Cantors) Let us bless the Lord.

R. (All) Thanks be to God.

V. (Presider) May the souls of the faithful departed, through the mercy of God, rest in peace.

R. (All) Amen.

The Presider prays the Prayer after the Office, and the Choirs respond

The Hours of Our Lady

None

Kneel

(Silently) O *divine and adorable Lord Jesus Christ, who has graciously redeemed us by thy bitter passion and death, we offer up this hour of None to thy honor and glory, and most humbly beseech thee, through the torments and agony thou didst suffer when hanging for three hours on the cross, and through thy precious death, which gave redemption and life to the world, and thy sacred burial, to grant us thy divine assistance, and the grace of the holy sacraments at our last hour and agony, and to give us a happy death, precious in thy sight, and pure from the least defilement of sin, that we may be at our death attended by thy holy angels, and by them borne up on high into those blissful regions, where we will contemplate thy divinity forevermore. Amen.*

Stand

+ **Hail Mary**, full of grace, the Lord is with thee. Blessed art thou among women, and blessed is the fruit of thy womb, Jesus. Holy Mary, mother of God, pray for us sinners, now, and in the hour of our death. Amen.

V. (Presider) Incline unto my aid, + O God.

R. O Lord, + make haste to help me.

(Profound bow) Glory be to the Father, and to the Son, and to the Holy Ghost. As it was in the beginning, is now, and ever shall be, world without end. Amen, *Alleluia.*

From Vespers on Saturday before the ninth Sunday before Easter (Septuagesima Sunday) till None on the Saturday after Easter, instead of Alleluia is said:

Praise be to thee, O Lord, king of eternal glory.

The first Cantor begins the hymn, and his Choir continues it; the second strophe is said by the opposite Choir, and so on. At the last strophe, both Choirs combine, and bow profoundly

Remember Thou Creator Lord

Memento, rerum Conditor

1

Memento Rerum Conditor

Me- men - to, re - rum Con - di - tor, nos-
Ma- ri - a Ma - ter gra - ti - ae, Dul-
Je - su ti - bi sit glo - ri - a, qui

tri quod o - lim cor - -po-ris, Sa- cra - ta_ab al - vo
cis Pa- rens cle- men - -ti-ae, tu nos ab hos - te
na - tus es de Vir - -gi-ne, Cum Pa - tre_et al - mo

Vir - gi - nis, Nas- cen - do, for - mam sum - -pse-ris
pro - te - ge, Et mor - tis ho - ra sus - -ci - pe
Spi - ri - tu In sem - pi - ter - na sae - -cu - la

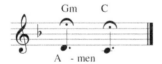

A - men

105

Anthem

If prayed in a Church, the Cantors rise and genuflect to the altar, go to the lectern, salute their Choirs, and the first Cantor recites the Anthem standing

(Through the year) Thou art fair and beautiful, O daughter of Jerusalem, formidable as an army in battle array.

(In Advent) Behold the handmaid of the Lord: be it done unto me according to thy word.

(Christmas time) Behold, Mary hath borne to us the Savior, whom John seeing, cried out: Behold the Lamb of God, behold him, who taketh away the sins of the world, alleluia.

Psalm 126

The people of God rejoice at their delivery from captivity

When the Lord brings back the captives of Sion, *we shall be like men cheered with comfort.

(Sit) Then shall our voices break forth in joyful praises, *and our tongue in canticles of jubilee.

Then shall they declare to their neighbors, *that the Lord hath done great things for them.

The Lord hath done great things for us, *we are therefore become joyful.

Bring back, O Lord, our captive people, *like a torrent in the south.

They who sow in tears *shall reap in joy.

They went forth shedding tears, *while they were sowing seeds.

But they will return full of joy, *bringing in the sheaves they have gathered.

(Profound bow) Glory be to the Father, and to the Son, and to the Holy Ghost. *As it was in the beginning, is now, and ever shall be, world without end. Amen, *Alleluia*.

Psalm 127

Man can do nothing without God

Unless the Lord himself shall build up the house, *they toil in vain who strive to build it.

Unless the Lord shall guard the city, *the sentinel doth watch in vain.

It is useless for you to rise before the light, *arise after you have taken rest, you who eat the bread of sorrow.

Since he will give sleep to his beloved ones: *know that children are blessings from the Lord, and that a numerous offspring is also a reward.

Like arrows in the hand of a powerful man, *are the children of those, who have been reproved.

Blessed is the man, whose desires are accomplished in them, *he shall not be confounded, when he shall speak to his enemies before the courts.

(Profound bow) Glory be to the Father, and to the Son, and to the Holy Ghost. *As it was in the beginning, is now, and ever shall be, world without end. Amen, *Alleluia.*

Psalm 128
The happiness of the just

Blessed are all who fear the Lord, *who walk according to his ways.

Because thou shalt partake of the labor of thy own hands, *thou art happy, and replenished with all good things.

Thy wife shall be like a fruitful vine, *in a garden at the rear of thy house.

Thy children, like young olive plants, *all round thy table.

Behold, thus shall the man be blessed, *who feareth the Lord.

May the Lord bless thee from Sion: *and mayest thou see the prosperity of Jerusalem all the days of thy life.

And mayest thou see the sons of thy children, *and peace given to Israel.

(Profound bow) Glory be to the Father, and to the Son, and to the Holy Ghost. *As it was in the beginning, is now, and ever shall be, world without end. Amen, *Alleluia.*

(Through the year) Thou art fair and beautiful, O daughter of Jerusalem, formidable as an army in battle array.

(In Advent) Behold the handmaid of the Lord: be it done unto me according to thy word.

(Christmas time) Behold, Mary hath borne to us the Savior, whom John seeing, cried out: Behold the Lamb of God, behold him, who taketh away the sins of the world, alleluia.

The Little Chapter through the year, except in Advent

Sirach 24:20
Douay Rheims 1900 American Version

V. (Presider) I yielded forth a fragrant perfume in the streets, like cinnamon and aromatic balm: and, like the best myrrh, I spread around the sweetest odor.

R. (All) Thanks be to God.

The Little Chapter In Advent

Isaiah 7:14

(Presider) Behold, a virgin shall conceive, and bring forth a son, and his name shall be called Emmanuel. He shall eat butter and honey, that he may know how to reject evil, and choose the good.

R. (All) Thanks be to God.

V. (Presider) After childbirth thou didst remain a pure virgin.

R. (All) O Mother of God, intercede for us.

(First Choir) Lord, have mercy on us.

(Second Choir) Christ, have mercy on us.

(All) Lord, have mercy on us.

V. (Cantors) O Lord, hear my prayer.

R. (All) And let my cry come unto thee.

Let us pray
Presider

(Through the year) Pardon, we beseech thee, O Lord, the sins of thy servants: that we, who are not able to please thee by our own actions, may be saved by the intercession of the mother of thy Son, our Lord: Who liveth and reigneth with thee and the Holy Ghost, one God, world without end.

R. (All) Amen.

(In Advent) O God, who was pleased that thy eternal Word, when the angel delivered his message, should take flesh in the womb of the blessed Virgin Mary, give ear to our humble petitions, and grant that we who believe her to be truly the mother of God, may be helped by her prayers. Through the same Lord Jesus Christ, thy Son, who liveth and reigneth with thee and the Holy Ghost, one God, world without end.

R. Amen.

(Christmas time) O God, who, by the fruitful virginity of blessed Mary, has given to mankind the rewards of eternal salvation: grant, we beseech thee, that we may experience her intercession for us, by whom we have received the Author of life, our Lord Jesus Christ, thy Son, who liveth and reigneth with thee and the Holy Ghost, one God, world without end.

R. (All) Amen.

V. (Cantors) O Lord, hear my prayer.

R. (All) And let my cry come unto thee.

V. (Cantors) Let us bless the Lord.

R. (All) Thanks be to God.

V. (Presider) May the souls of the faithful departed, through the mercy of God, rest in peace.

R. (All) Amen.

(In silence) **Our Father,** &c.

V. May the Lord grant us his peace.

R. And eternal life. Amen.

The Presider prays the Prayer after the Office, and the Choirs respond

Office for the Dead

The rubrics are the same throughout as for the Little Office

Vespers for the Dead

Traditionally, Vespers is the first office of the liturgical day. It was prayed in religious communities late in the afternoon, along with Compline. Today, it may be of more benefit for the laity to pray it at around 6 in the evening.

Kneel

O divine and adorable Lord Jesus Christ, who has graciously redeemed us by thy bitter passion and death, we offer up these Vespers to thy honor and glory, and most humbly beseech thee, through thy dolorous agony and bloody sweat which thou didst suffer in the garden, to grant us true contrition of heart, and sorrow for our sins, with a firm resolution never more to offend thee, but so satisfy thy divine justice for past iniquity. Amen.

The Presider taps to call everyone to prayer. Beginning with the Sign of the Cross, the Presider intones and all pray the Our Father in silence.

Stand

V. +**Our Father**, *etc. silently*...and lead us not into temptation.

R. (All) But deliver us from evil.

V. (Presider) Incline unto my aid, + O God.

R. (All) O Lord, make haste to help me.

(Profound bow) Glory be to the Father, and to the Son, and to the Holy Ghost. *As it was in the beginning, is now, and ever shall be, world without end. Amen

The first Cantor stands and recites the appropriate Anthem and the first half line of the Psalm; the second Choir takes up the second half of the line, then the Choirs alternate

Anthem
I will please the Lord in the land of the living.

Psalm 116

I have loved the Lord, because he will hear *the voice of my prayer.

For he hath inclined his ear to me: *I will therefore invoke him all the days of my life.

The sorrows of death have encompassed me *and the perils of hell have rushed upon me.

I am sunk in distress and grief: *and I called on the name of the Lord.

O Lord, deliver my soul: *the Lord is merciful and righteous and our God is full of compassion.

The Lord taketh care of the little ones: *I humbled myself, and he delivered me.

Seek for thy true repose, O my soul: *for the Lord hath bestowed on thee many blessings.

For he hath saved my soul from death: *he hath dried the tears from my eyes and preserved me from falling.

I will please the Lord *in the land of the living.

Eternal rest *grant to them, O Lord.

And may the perpetual light of glory *shine upon them.

Anthem: I will please the Lord in the land of the living.

Anthem

How miserable I am, O Lord, that my exile is so prolonged!

Psalm 120

I cried out to the Lord in my extreme distress, *and he graciously heard me.

O Lord, deliver my soul from unjust lips, *and from a deceitful tongue.

What shall be done to thee, or what punishment shalt thou receive, *for thy deceitful tongue?

Thou shalt feel the sharp arrows of the mighty, *accompanied with destructive burning coals.

How miserable I am that my exile is so prolonged! I dwell here among the inhabitants of Cedar, *my soul hath been long a sojourner.

I was peaceable with those who hated peace, *when I spoke to them they opposed me without any cause.

Eternal rest *grant to them, O Lord.

And may the perpetual light of glory *shine upon them.

Anthem. How miserable I am, O Lord, that my exile is so prolonged.

Anthem

The Lord preserved thee from all evil, may the Lord still protect thy soul.

Psalm 121

I lifted up my eyes towards the mountains, *from whence I expect assistance

My help is from the Lord, *who made heaven and earth.

May he not suffer thy foot to be moved, *neither may he slumber who is thy guardian.

Behold, he shall neither slumber nor sleep, *that keepeth Israel.

The Lord watcheth over thee, the Lord is thy protector, *he is at thy right hand.

The sun shall not burn thee by day, *nor shall the moon molest thee by night.

The Lord preserveth thee from all evil, *may the Lord still protect thy soul.

May the Lord watch over thee coming in and going out, *now and for evermore.

Eternal rest *grant to them, O Lord.

And may the perpetual light of glory *shine upon them.

Anthem. The Lord preserved thee from all evil, may the Lord still protect thy soul.

Anthem

If thou wilt consider our iniquities, O mighty Lord, who shall endure it?

Psalm 130

From the depths I have cried out to thee, *O gracious Lord, hear my voice

Let thy ears be attentive *to the words of my petition.

If thou wilt consider our iniquities, O mighty Lord, *who shall endure it?

But with thee there is merciful forgiveness, *and by reason of thy law I have waited on thee, O Lord.

My soul hath relied on his word, *my soul hath hoped in the

Lord.

From the morning watch even until night, *let Israel hope in the Lord.

Because with the Lord there is mercy, *and with him is plentiful redemption.

And he shall redeem Israel *from all his iniquities.

Eternal rest grant to them, O Lord.

*And may the perpetual light of glory shine upon them.

Anthem. If thou wilt consider our iniquities, O mighty Lord, who shall endure it?

Anthem

Do not despise the works of thy own hands.

Psalm 138

I will praise thee, O Lord, with my whole heart, *because thou hast attended to the words of my mouth.

In presence of the angels will I sing to thee, *I will adore thee in thy holy temple, and praise thy name.

In grateful remembrance of thy mercy and of thy truth, *for thou hast magnified thy holy name above all other names.

In what day so ever I shall call on thee, graciously hear me, *thou wilt increase the sanctity of my soul.

May all the kings of the earth, O Lord, celebrate thy praises, *for they have heard all thy sacred words.

And may they sing in the ways of the Lord, *for the glory of the Lord is very great.

For the Lord is most high, and regards the low things, *and the high he knoweth afar off.

If I should walk in the midst of dangers, thou wilt preserve my life, *for thou hast exerted thy power against the wrath of my enemies, and thy right hand hath saved me.

The Lord will avenge my cause, *O Lord, thy mercies are eternal, do not despise the works of thy own hands.

Eternal rest *grant to them, O Lord.

And may the perpetual light of glory *shine upon them.

Anthem: Do not despise the works of thy own hands.

V. I have heard a voice from heaven saying to me:

R. Blessed are the dead, who repose in the Lord.

Anthem

Whatever my Father giveth me shall come to me, and him who cometh to me I will not reject.

Canticle of the Blessed Virgin Mary
Luke 1:46

My soul doth magnify the Lord, and my spirit hath rejoiced *in God my Savior.

Because he hath regarded the humility of his handmaid, *behold from henceforth all generations shall call me blessed.

For he who is mighty hath done great things to me, *and holy is his name.

And his mercy is from generation to generation *to those who fear him.

He hath shown might in his arm, *he hath scattered the proud in the conceit of their heart.

He hath cast down the mighty from their seat, *and hath exalted the humble.

He hath filled the hungry with good things, *and the rich he hath sent away empty.

He hath received Israel his servant, *being mindful of his mercy.

As he spoke to our Fathers, *to Abraham and his seed forever.

Eternal rest *grant to them, O Lord.

And may the perpetual light of glory *shine upon them.

Anthem. Whatever my Father giveth me, shall come to me, and I will not reject him who cometh to me.

Our Father, *in silence.*

V. And lead us not into temptation

R. But deliver us from evil.

The Versicles and Prayers are at the bottom of p. 141

.

Matins for the Dead

To be said in a double rite with the Invitatory and three Nocturns, on the days of decease and burial, on the third, seventh, and thirtieth days after death, on the anniversary day, and when the office is solemnly celebrated in choir. The Anthems are said in choir before and after the Psalms; the Psalm From the Depths, at the end of the Lauds, is omitted, and only one Prayer is recited with the long conclusion. These remarks are also to be observed at Vespers.

Kneel

(Silently) *O Divine and adorable Lord Jesus Christ, who have graciously redeemed us by your bitter passion and death, we offer up these Matins and Lauds to your honor and glory, and most humbly beseech you, through the vile treatment you received from the Jews, who dragged you to the courts of impious High priests, where you were falsely accused, struck in the face, called a blasphemer, and declared guilty of death, and suffered most cruel torments with blows, bruises, and unheard-of injuries, during the whole night, to grant us resignation and silence during all calumnies, detractions, and sufferings for the love of you, and to give us grace never to return injury for injury, but to practice that truly Christian revenge of overcoming evil with good, to do good to those who hate us, to bless those who curse us, and to pray for those who persecute and calumniate us: Amen.*

The Presider calls everyone to prayer. Beginning with the Sign of the Cross, intoned by the Presider, all pray the Our Father in silence.

Stand

V. + **Our Father,** etc. *in silence* ...and lead us not into temptation

R. (All) But deliver us from evil.

V. (Presider) O Lord, + open thou my lips.

R. (All) And my mouth shall declare thy praise

V. (Presider) Incline unto my aid, + O God.

R. (All) O Lord, make haste to help me.

(Profound bow) Glory be to the Father, and to the Son, and to the Holy Ghost. *As it was in the beginning, is now, and ever shall be, world without end. Amen

115

Invitatory

Anthem

(Cantors) Come, let us adore the Lord, our King, who giveth life to all things.

(All) Come, let us adore the Lord, our King, who giveth life to all things.

Psalm 95

An invitation to praise God, and to obey Him

Come, let us rejoice in the Lord, *let us joyfully cry out to God our Savior,

Let us present ourselves before him to celebrate his praises, *and with canticles of jubilee let us sing to him.

Come, let us adore the Lord, our King, *who giveth life to all things.

Because God is a mighty Lord *and a great King above all gods.

The Lord will not reject his people; *in his hands are all the bounds of the earth,

And he looks down on the heights of the mountains, *who giveth life to all things.

The sea is his, for he made it, *and his hands framed the earth.

(Genuflect)

Come then, let us adore and fall prostrate before God, *let us weep in the presence of the Lord who made us,

Because he is the Lord our God; *we are his people, and the sheep of his pasture.

Come, let us adore the Lord our King, *who giveth life to all things.

If this day you should hear his voice, *harden not your hearts,

As you did when you provoked him on the day you offended him in the desert, *where your Fathers tempted me, they tried and saw my works. Who giveth life to all things.

I was forty years with this race of men, and said: *The hearts of this people are always straying, but they have not known my ways,

And I swore to them in my wrath, *that they should not enter the abode of my rest.

Come, let us adore the Lord our King, *who giveth life to all things.

Eternal rest *grant to them, O Lord.

And may the perpetual light of glory *shine upon them.

Anthem. Come, let us adore the Lord our King, who giveth life to all things.

First Nocturn

Anthem

Guide my steps, O Lord my God, to walk in thy presence.

Psalm 5

Give ear to my words, O Lord, *and listen to my supplications.

Be attentive to the voice of my prayer, *O my King and my God.

For to thee will I address my prayer, *thou, O Lord, in the morning wilt hearken to my voice.

At the dawn of the day I shall present myself before thee, *and will consider that thou art not a God who lovest iniquity.

The wicked shall not abide near thee, *nor shall the unjust remain in thy presence.

Thou dost hate all those who commit evil things, *and dost destroy all who speak lying words.

The Lord will abominate the bloody and deceitful man, *but as for me, in the abundance of thy mercy,

I will enter thy house *and full of respectful awe will adore thee in thy holy temple.

O Lord, lead me in the paths of righteousness, *and on account of my enemies guide my steps to walk in thy presence.

For truth is not in their words, *and their hearts are vain.

Their throats are an open sepulcher, they used their tongues to deceive, *judge them thou, O God.

Let them fail in their designs; reject them for their great and manifold crimes, *for it is thee, O Lord, they have provoked.

And let all rejoice who hope in thee: *they shall eternally exult and thou shalt abide among them.

And all who love thy holy name shall be glorified, *for thou wilt bless the righteous.

O Lord, thou hast protected us with a shield, *for the tender love thou dost bear unto us.

Eternal rest *grant to them, O Lord.

And may the perpetual light of glory *shine upon them.

Anthem. Guide my steps, O Lord my God, to walk in thy presence.

Anthem

Incline to me, O Lord, and deliver my soul, for in death there is no one mindful of thee.

Psalm 6

Lord, rebuke me not in thy fury, *nor chastise me in thy wrath.

Take pity on me, O Lord, for I am very weak, *heal me, O Lord, for a tremor has seized my bones.

And my soul is greatly troubled, *but how long, O Lord, wilt thou delay to help me?

Incline to me, O Lord, and deliver my soul; *save me for thy mercy's sake.

For in death there is no one mindful of thee, *and in hell who shall declare thy praises?

I am tired in sighing to thee, I will every night wash my bed with weeping, *and will water my couch with my tears.

My eyes are sorely affected by the rage of my foes; *I am grown old amidst all my enemies.

Depart from me, all you who commit iniquity, *for the Lord hath graciously heard the plaints of my weeping.

The Lord hath graciously heard my petition; *the Lord hath attended to my prayer.

May all my enemies blush and be greatly troubled, *let them be put to speedy flight and covered with shame.

Eternal rest *grant to them, O Lord.

And may the perpetual light of glory *shine upon them.

Anthem. Incline to me, O Lord, and deliver my soul, for in death there is no one mindful of thee.

Anthem

Protect me, lest the enemy seize on my soul, like a lion, while there is none to rescue or to save me.

Psalm 7

O Lord, my God, in thee have I put my trust; *save me from all who persecute me, and deliver me from their hands.

Protect me, lest the enemy seize on my soul, like a lion, *where there is none to rescue or to save me

O Lord, my God, if I have committed what they charge me with, *if my hands are sullied with iniquity;

If I have rendered evil to them who did me harm, *I deserve to be despoiled of everything by my enemies.

Let the enemy persecute my soul and seize me, and let him trample me on the earth, and deprive me of life, *and bring down my glory to the very dust.

Arise then, O Lord, in thy wrath, *and exert thy anger in the land of my enemies.

Arise, I pray, O Lord my God, according to the command thou hast given, *and multitudes of people shall come around thee.

Resume the functions of justice on thy high tribunal, *the Lord judgeth the nations.

Judge me, O Lord, according to my righteousness, *and according to my innocence.

The wickedness of sinners shall be destroyed, and thou wilt conduct the righteous, *thou, O God who searchest the hearts and reins.

It is just I should expect my help from the Lord, *who saveth the upright of heart.

God is a just judge, mighty and patient *doth he every day exert his wrath?

Unless you be truly converted to him, he will brandish his sword, *he has bent his bow and got the quiver ready.

And in it he has fixed deadly darts: *he hath prepared fiery arrows.

Behold, the wicked man conceived unjust designs, *he contrived tortures, and brought forth iniquity.

He opened a pit, and dug it up, *but has himself fallen into the calamity which he had prepared for others.

The sorrow he intended for me shall return upon his own head, *and his wickedness shall be visited upon himself.

I will praise the Lord for his justice, *I will sing praises to the name of the most high Lord.

Eternal rest grant to them, O Lord.

*And may the perpetual light of glory shine upon them.

Anthem. Protect me, lest the enemy seize on my soul, like a lion, while there is none rescue or to save me.

V. From the gates of hell.

R. Deliver their souls, O Lord.

Our father, etc., *all in silence.*

First Lesson
Job 7

V. (Presider) Spare me, O Lord, for my days are nothing. What is man to merit thy esteem? Or why dost thou place thy affections upon him? Thou dost visit him early with consolations, and then triest him with sudden afflictions. When wilt thou have compassion on me, and give me some ease, even for a moment? I have sinned against thee: what shall I therefore do, O guardian of man, to appease thy wrath? Why dost thou regard me as thy enemy, and render me a burthen to myself? Why dost thou not pardon me my sins, and cleanse me from my iniquities? Behold me now dying to be buried in the earth, and if thou sleekest me in the morning, I shall not be alive.

R. I firmly believe that my Redeemer is living, and that I shall rise again from the earth on the last day, *and that in my own flesh I shall see God, my Savior.

V. Whom I myself in my own person shall see, and with my own eyes contemplate.

R. And that in my own flesh I shall see God, My Savior.

Second Lesson
Job 10

My soul is weary of life. I will speak of myself, and in the bitterness of my soul. I will say to God: Do not condemn me, tell me what have I done to deserve such punishment. Doth it seem good to thee to calumniate and oppress me, who am the work of thy hands, and to favor the designs of the wicked against me? Hast thou thy eyes of flesh, or wilt thou see as man doth? Are thy days as the days of man? Or are thy years like ours, which glide away? That thou shouldst examine my iniquities, and search my sins: thou knowest that I have done no evil thing, whereas no one could rescue me out of thy hands.

R. Thou didst raise Lazarus, fetid from the grave. O Lord, grant to them a place of rest and of comfort.

V. Thou art come to judge the living and the dead, and to consume the whole world by fire.

R. O Lord, grant to them a place of rest and of comfort.

Third lesson
Job 10

Thy hands, O Lord, have created me, and have formed me in every part, and wilt thou now precipitate me into ruin? Remember, I beseech thee, that thou hast made me from the slime of earth, and that thou wilt make me return again to dust. Hast thou not extracted me from these raw material, and formed me, as milk is coagulated, and made into cheese? Thou didst clothe me with skin and flesh, and with bones and sinews didst strengthen my frame. Thou didst grant me life, through thy great mercy, and thy watchful care hath ever since preserved me.

R. O Lord, when thou shalt come to judge the world, where shall I hide myself from the view of thy wrath? *For I have sinned exceedingly during my life.

V. I am seized with fear at my offences, and I blush for shame before thee: do not condemn me, when thou shalt come to judge.

R. For I have sinned exceedingly during my life.

Eternal rest grant to them, O Lord. *And may the perpetual light of glory shine upon them.

R. For I have sinned exceedingly during my life.

Second Nocturn

Anthem

In a place of pasture he hath settled me.

Psalm 23

The Lord taketh care of me, and I shall want for nothing *in a place of pasture he hath settled me.

He hath brought me up near refreshing waters *he hath inclined my soul to virtue.

He hath conducted me through the paths of righteousness *for the glory of his name.

For if I should have to walk even amidst the shades of death, I would fear no evil *for thou art with me.

Thy rod and thy staff *have been my protection and comfort.

Thou hast prepared for me a banquet *to strengthen me against my enemies who persecute me.

Thou hast spread on my head perfuming oil *and on, how excellently good is the wine I drink!

Thou wilt grant me thy great mercy *all the days of my life:

That I may dwell in the blissful mansions of the Lord *for all eternity.

Eternal rest grant to them, O Lord.

*And may the perpetual light of glory shine upon them.

Anthem. In a place of pasture he hath settled me.

Anthem

Remember not, O Lord, the faults of my youth and sins of ignorance.

Psalm 25

To thee, O Lord, Have I lifted up my soul, *in thee, my God, I place my trust, let me not be put to shame.

Let my enemies not insult over me *for all those who hope in thee shall not be confounded.

Let all those be filled with shame *who wantonly commit injustices.

O Lord, make known to me thy ways, *and instruct me in thy paths.

Guide me in thy truth, and teach me, *for thou art God my Savior, and I have waited on thee the whole day long.

Call to mind, O Lord, thy great compassion, *and thy manifold mercies which thou hast shown from the beginning of creation.

Remember not the faults of my youth, *and my sins of ignorance.

Be mindful of me according to thy mercy, *O Lord for thy goodness' sake.

The Lord is good and just; *he will therefore give to sinners his law, which they should follow.

He will guide the mild in justice, *he will teach the meek his ways.

All the ways of the Lord are mercy and truth, *to those who observe his law and his ordinances.

Through thy sacred name, O Lord, thou wilt mercifully pardon my sin, *which is exceeding great.

Who is the man who feareth the Lord? *He has appointed him a law in the way he has chosen.

His soul shall possess good things, *and his children shall inherit the land.

The Lord shall strengthen those who fear him, *and he shall manifest his alliance with them.

My eyes are ever raised toward the Lord, *for he will disengage my feet from the snare.

Look down, and have pity on me, *for I am forlorn and poor.

The afflictions of my heart are manifold, *deliver me from the necessities to which I am reduced.

Cast an eye of compassion on my miseries and my sorrows, *and forgive me all my sins.

Consider how my enemies are multiplied, *and how unjust is the hatred they bear me.

Protect my soul, and deliver me from them, *I shall not be ashamed, because I have hoped in thee.

The innocent and the righteous have adhered to me, *because I have awaited on thee.

Deliver Israel, O God, *from all its tribulations.

Eternal rest grant to them, O Lord.

*And may the perpetual light of glory shine upon them.

Anthem. Remember now, O Lord, the faults of my youth, and my sins of ignorance.

Anthem

I hope to enjoy the good things of the Lord in the land of the living.

Psalm 27

The Lord is my light and my salvation, *whom shall I fear?

The Lord is the protector of my life, *who shall make me tremble?

Whilst the wicked draw near against me, *to devour my flesh,

Those very enemies who afflict me *are themselves become weak, and have fallen.

If whole armies were drawn up against me, *my heart shall not fear.

If battle should rage against me, *I will still hope in the Lord.

I have asked one favor of the Lord, and will persevere in my petition, *to dwell in the house of the Lord all the days of my life.

That I may contemplate the loveliness of the Lord, *and

frequent his sacred temple.

For he hath concealed me in his tabernacle, *in the days of my afflictions he hath protected me in the secret recesses of his abode.

He hath exalted me upon a rock, *and now again he hath raised my head above my enemies.

I went round his altar, and have offered up in his temple a sacrifice of praise. *I will sing canticles and hymns to the Lord.

O Lord, mercifully hear my petition which I have earnestly presented to thee: *have mercy on me and graciously hear me.

My heart hath wished, my eyes have longed for thee; *thy presence, O Lord, I will still desire to see.

Turn not away thy countenance from me, *do not depart in wrath from thy servant.

Be thou my helper, *do not forsake or slight me, O God who art my Savior.

For my father and my mother have abandoned me, *but the Lord hath taken me under his care.

Show me, O Lord, the law of thy ways, *and direct me in the right path on account of my enemies.

Deliver me not over to the will of those who persecute me, *because false witnesses have stood up against me, but their iniquity belied itself.

I hope to enjoy the good things of the Lord *in the land of the living.

Wait on the Lord, be of good courage: *let thy heart be resolute, and wait patiently on the Lord.

Eternal rest grant to them, O Lord. *And may the perpetual light of glory shine upon them.

Anthem. I hope to enjoy the good things of the Lord in the land of the living.

V. May the Lord place them with princes.

R. With the princes of his people.

Our Father, *all in silence.*

Fourth Lesson
Job 12

Tell me, O Lord, how great are my iniquities and sins, my evil deeds and offences discover me. Why dost thou withdraw from me thy compassionate regards, and treat me as thy enemy? Against a leaf that is carried away by the wind, thou exertest thy might, and pursuest a withered straw. Thou writest against me bitter charges, and seemest to oppress me with the sins of my youth. Thou hast, as it were, fettered my feet, thou hast scrutinized my actions, and all my footsteps thou hast examined. Thus thou treatest me, whom am soon to fall into corruption, and to become like a garment eaten up by the moths.

R. Remember me, O God, for my life is like the fleeting wind. *The eyes of man shall soon cease to behold me.

V. From the depths I have cried to thee, O gracious Lord, hear my voice.

R. The eyes of man shall soon cease to behold me.

Fifth Lesson
Job 14

Man born of a woman liveth but a short time, and is burthened with many miseries. He is likened to a flower which is nipped as soon as it comes forth; he disappears like a shadow, and never continues in the same state. And deignest thou to cast thy eyes on such a being, and to cite him in judgment? Who can make pure and righteous him that was conceived in iniquity? Art not thou who alone canst do it? The days of man are short, thou hast fixed the number of his months, and hast prescribed the term of his life, which he cannot go beyond. Cease then a little to afflict him, that he may rest until the wished for day come to him, as to the hired servant, for receiving his wages.

R. Woe to me, O Lord, for I have grievously sinned during my life! What shall I do, unhappy wretch? Whither shall I flee, but to thee, O my God? *Have mercy on me when thou comest at the last day.

V. My soul is deeply troubled: do thou, O Lord, afford it comfort.

R. Have mercy on me, when thou comest at the last day.

Sixth Lesson
Job 14

Who will petition for me the favor, that thou mayest place me in the lower recesses of the earth, and hide me there, till thy wrath be appeased, and that thou mayest fix a time when thou wilt remember me in thy great mercy? Dost thou think that a dead man can rise to life again? I shall therefore patiently wait all the days of my warfare, till I receive from thy goodness the grace of a perfect change. Thou wilt call me, and I shall answer, thou wilt stretch forth thy saving arm to the work of thy own hands. Thou hast indeed witnessed the evil actions of my life; but mercifully pardon my sins.

R. Remember not my sins, O Lord: *When thou shalt come to judge the world with fire.

V. Guide my steps, O Lord my God, to walk in thy presence.

R. When thou shalt come to judge the world by fire.

Eternal rest grant to them, O Lord.

*And may the perpetual light of glory shine upon them.

R. When thou shalt come to judge the world by fire.

Third Nocturn

Anthem

Be pleased, O Lord, to deliver me; Lord graciously look to me and help me.

Psalm 40

I have waited on the Lord with earnest expectation, *and he hath heard me.

He hath attended to my prayers, *and hath drawn me out of a pit of misery, and out of the filthy mire.

He hath placed my feet upon a rock, *and guided my footsteps.

He hath put a new song in my mouth, *a song of jubilee to our God.

Many shall see this with awful fear, *and shall place their hope in the Lord.

Blessed is the man whose hope is in the name of the Lord, *and who hath not regard to vanities and to deceitful follies.

Thou hast wrought many wonders, O Lord, my God, *and in thy designs there is none like to thee.

I have endeavored to relate them and to speak of them, *but they are above number.

Thou wert not satisfied with sacrifice and oblation, *but hast pierced my ears to become thy servant.

Burnt offerings and sin offerings were not what thou calledst for, *then said I: Behold, I come.

It is decreed for me at the head of the book, that I should do thy will, *I have desired it, O Lord, and thy law is engraven in my heart.

I have announced thy justice in the congregation of many people, *behold I have not kept silence; thou, O Lord, dost truly know it.

I did not conceal thy righteousness within my own breast, *but have published thy truth and thy saving mercy.

I have not concealed thy mercy nor thy truth *from the numerous assembly.

Do not withdraw, O Lord, thy tender mercies from me; *thy mercy and thy truth have always protected me.

For evils without number have encompassed me, *I am so overladen with iniquities that I cannot see to know them.

They are multiplied above the hairs of my head, *for which my heart fainteth away.

Be pleased, O Lord, to deliver me. *Lord, graciously look to me and help me.

Let all be branded with confusion and shame, *who seek to take away my life.

Let them be put to flight and ignominy, *who desire evils to me.

Let them immediately fall into the contempt which they deserve, *who insult me with derision.

Let all who seek thee exult and rejoice in thee, *and let those who love thy saving mercy ever cry out: May the Lore be glorified.

For though I am needy and poor, *the Lord taketh care of me.

Thou art my helper and my protector, *God, do not delay to assist me.

Eternal rest grant to them, O Lord.

*And may the perpetual light of glory shine upon them.

Anthem. Be pleased, O Lord, to deliver me; Lord, graciously look to me and assist me.

Anthem
Heal my soul, O Lord, for I have sinned against thee.

Psalm 40
Blessed is the man who hath compassion on the needy and the poor, *in the evil day the Lord will protect him.

May the Lord preserve him and grant him life and make him

blessed on earth, *and deliver him not up to the will of his enemies.

May the Lord help him when on the bed of sorrow, *thou hast shaken well and fixed his bed for ease in sickness.

I said: Thou, O Lord, have mercy on me, *heal my soul for I have sinned against thee.

My enemies have spoken evil things against me, *When will he die? And when shall his name perish?

If anyone came in to visit me, he spoke deceitfully, *and his heart was full of iniquity.

He went out, *and conspired with the others to my prejudice.

All my enemies whispered together against me, *they devised evil machinations against me.

An unjust design they formed against me, *but will not he who sleeps rise again?

For the man in whom I found peace and placed my confidence, *who even partook of my bread at table, he hath shown great treachery to me.

But thou, O Lord, take pity on me and resuscitate me, *that I may render to them what they deserve.

I have known thou lovest me and dost wish me well *because thou wilt not permit the enemy to insult over me.

Thou hast taken care of me on account of my innocence, *and hast settled me always in thy presence.

May the Lord God of Israel be ever blessed for endless ages, *so be it, so be it.

Eternal rest grant to them, O Lord.

*And may the perpetual light of glory shine upon them.

Anthem. Heal my soul, O Lord, for I have sinned against thee.

Anthem

My soul is inflamed with an ardent desire to enjoy the mighty and living God. When shall I come to possess the vision of the Lord?

Psalm 42

As the hart panteth after the fountains of water, *so does my soul thirst after thee, O God.

My soul is inflamed with an ardent desire to enjoy the mighty and living God. *When shall I come to possess the vision of the Lord?

My tears have been my bread both day and night, *whilst they daily say: Where is now thy God?

I have remembered these things, and have been much affected with my soul, *for I shall go over into the place of a most wonderful dwelling, even into the blissful mansions of God.

Amidst the voices of jubilee and thanksgiving, *like the rejoicings of a sumptuous banquet.

Why art thou then sorrowful, O my soul? *and why art thou so disturbed?

Hope in God, for I will still praise him *he is the Savior I sought for, and my God.

My soul is interiorly troubled *I will therefore remember thee from the mountains of Hermon, and from the hills.

One abyss of calamities hath called another after it *with the roarings of thy cataracts.

All thy surges, and thy billows *have passed over me.

The Lord hath shown his mercy to me day by day *and at night I have sung to him a canticle of praise.

I will pray to the God of my life, *and I will say to him: Thou art my protector.

Why hast thou been unmindful of me? *And why do I go sorrowful, while the enemy doth afflict me?

While I am tortured and destroyed, *my enemies who afflict me insult over me.

Whilst every day they say to me: Where is now thy God? *Why art thou sorrowful, O my soul? And why art thou so disturbed?

Hope in God, for I will continue to praise him. *He is the Savior I sought for, and he is my God.

Eternal rest grant to them, O Lord.

*And may the perpetual light of glory *shine upon them.

Anthem. My soul is inflamed with an ardent desire to enjoy the mighty and living God: When shall I come to possess the vision of the Lord?

V. Deliver not to beasts the souls of those who praise thee.

R. And continue not to reject the souls of the poor.

Our Father, *all in silence.*

Seventh Lesson
Job 17

My spirit is quite spent, my days are shortened, and there

remains nothing for me but the grave. I have not sinned, and yet, through affliction, my eyes are drowned in bitter tears. Deliver me, O Lord, and place me under thy care, and I shall not then fear, whosoever may fight against me. My days have gone by, my thoughts are dissipated, and afflict my heart. They have changed night into day, and when darkness comes, I long for light. If I wait, my dwelling shall be the grave, and I shall strew my bed in that darksome prison. I have said to rottenness, thou art my father; and to the worms, you are my mother and sister. Where then is my hope, and who hath regard to my patience?

R. Whilst I am sinning daily, and not repenting, the fear of death disturbs me greatly: *O God, since out of hell there is no redemption, have mercy on me and save me.

V. Save me, O God, through thy sacred name, and rescue me by thy power.

R. O God, since out of hell there is no redemption, have mercy on me and save me.

Eighth Lesson
Job 19

My flesh is entirely consumed, my bones are only covered with skin, and emaciated lips are left about my teeth. Take pity on me, at least you, my friends, take pity, for the anger of the Lord has heavily fallen upon me. Why do you add to the afflictions with which God has visited me? Why do you seem to glut yourselves with the sufferings of my flesh? Who will grant me to write down what I am going to say? Who will permit me to imprint these my words in a plate of lead, with an iron style, or to engrave them on flint with a pencil of steel? I know that my Redeemer is living, that I shall rise again from the earth on the last day, that I shall be clothed again with my skin, and that in my own flesh I shall see my God: whom I myself in my own person shall see, and with my own eyes shall contemplate. This, my confident hope, is carefully laid up in my heart.

R. Do not judge me, O Lord, according to my deeds, for I have done nothing to merit thy approbation: therefore I humbly entreat thy divine majesty: *That thou, O God, wilt forgive me all my iniquity.

V. Wash me, O Lord, still more from my guilt, and cleanse from the stains of sin.

R. That thou, O God, wilt forgive me all my iniquity.

Ninth Lesson
Job 10

Who, O Lord, didst thou give me birth? Oh, that I had been consumed before the eyes of man could see my wretched condition! Oh that I had been as if I did not exist, hurried from the womb to the grave. Will not my few days be shortly ended? Permit me, therefore, to give vent to my grief for a little while, before I go to the darksome land, from whence there is no return; a land which is covered with the shades of death; a land of misery and obscurity, where the shades of death and no order, but everlasting horror, have their settled abode.

R. Deliver me, O Lord, from eternal death on that dreadful day, *when the heavens and earth shall be moved. *Whilst thou wilt come to judge the world by fire.

V. I am seized with trembling and dread, while I reflect on the rigorous examination and the vengeful wrath of that day.

R. When the heavens and earth shall be moved.

V. That day shall be a day of wrath, calamity, and misery: the great day of extreme bitterness and terror.

R. Whilst thou wilt come to judge the world by fire.

Eternal rest grant to them, O Lord, *and may perpetual light shine upon them.

R. Deliver me, O Lord, from eternal death on that dreadful day, when the heavens and earth shall be moved, whilst thou wilt come to judge the world by fire.

Mark. – In this foregoing Responsory, at the end of the first Versicle is repeated that part of the Responsory only which is included between the two asterisks; after the second Versicle is said the remainder of the Responsory from the last asterisk, and after the third Versicle the entire Responsory is again recited.
The above Responsory is always said when the office is of a double rite, but when the office is simple, that is, when only one Nocturn is said at Matins, the following is substituted:

R. Deliver me, O Lord, from the evil ways which lead to hell, thou who didst break down its brazen gates, who didst descend into Limbo, to visit the faithful souls there, and didst give light to behold thee to those: *Who were detained in darkness.

V. They cried out with joy, saying: Thou art at length come, O thou, our Redeemer.

R. Who were detained in darkness.

V. Eternal Rest grant to them, O Lord, and may the light of glory shine upon them.

R. Who were detained in darkness.

Lauds for the Dead

Anthem

The bones that are humbled shall rejoice in the Lord.

Psalm 1

Have mercy on me O God, *according to thy great mercy.

And according to the multitude of thy tender mercies, *blot out my iniquity.

Wash me yet more from my iniquity, *and cleanse me from my sin.

For I know my iniquity, *and my sin is always against me.

To thee alone have I sinned, and have done what is evil in thy presence, *I acknowledge it, that thou mayest be justified in thy judgment, and mayest prevail in thy just sentence.

Behold, I was conceived in iniquities, *and in sins did my mother conceive me.

Thou hast loved truth, *and hast revealed to me the mysterious and hidden secrets of thy divine wisdom.

Thou wilt sprinkle me with hyssop, and I shall be cleansed, *thou wilt wash me, and I shall be made whiter than snow.

Thou wilt speak to me words of consolation and of joy, *and this wretched being of mine shall rejoice.

Turn away thy thoughts from my sins, *and cancel all my iniquities.

Render my heart pure and clean, O God, *and renew within me a spirit of righteousness.

Cast me not away from thy presence, *and take not thy holy Spirit from me.

Impart unto me the joy of thy salutary graces, *and strengthen me with the spirit of true piety.

I will teach the unjust thy ways, *and the wicked shall be converted to thee.

Deliver me from my crimes of blood, O great God, my Savior, *and my tongue shall joyfully proclaim thy justice.

O Lord, thou wilt open my lips, *and my tongue shall declare thy praise.

For if thou hadst desired a sacrifice, I would indeed have offered it up to thee, *with whole burnt offerings thou wilt not be well pleased.

The sacrifice which God requires, is a repentant spirit, *a contrite and humble heart, O God, thou wilt not despise.

Show thy kind will, O Lord, to Sion, *that the walls of Jerusalem may be built up.

Then wilt thou accept the sacrifices of righteousness, of oblations, and of whole burnt offerings, *then shall they immolate victims on thy altars.

Eternal rest grant to them, O Lord, *And may perpetual light shine upon them.

Anthem. The bones that are humbled shall rejoice in the Lord.

Anthem

O Lord, graciously hear my prayer, for all flesh shall return to thee.

Psalm 65

It is meet, O God, to praise thee in Sion, *and to render our vows to thee in Jerusalem.

Graciously hear my prayer, *for all flesh shall return to thee.

The words of the wicked have prevailed over us, *and thou wilt pardon our transgressions.

Blessed is he whom thou hast chosen, and taken to thyself, *he shall dwell in thy courts.

We shall be replenished with the good things of thy house, *thy temple is holy and wonderful in equity.

Graciously hear us, O God our Savior, *thou who art the hope of those who dwell at the confines of the earth, and in the most distant islands of the sea.

Thou, who didst establish the mountains by thy own strength, and in the exercise of thy power, *who excites the foaming billows of the sea, and calmest again the roaring of its waves.

Nations shall be dismayed, and the distant inhabitants of the earth shall be terrified at thy great prodigies, *thou shalt rejoice the world from the rising to the setting sun.

Thou hast visited the earth, and watered it with much rain, *thou hast enriched it to produce abundant fruit.

Thy great rivers are full of water, thou hast prepared food for thy people, *for thus the land is rendered fertile.

Fill plentifully the streams thereof, increase its produce, *the earth shall bring forth its fruit, and shall thus rejoice at the falling rain.

Thou shalt bountifully bless us with fruit the whole year round, *and the fields shall abound with plentiful produce.

The deserts too shall look beautiful with good pasture, *and the hilly parts shall seem to exult with joy.

The rams of the flocks shall be covered with fleece, and the valleys shall bear abundant corn, *the people shall unite in concerts of joy, yea they shall sing canticles of praise.

Eternal rest grant to them, O Lord, *And may perpetual light shine upon them.

Anthem. Thy right hand, O Lord, hath protected me.

Psalm 63

O God, my God, *I watch unto thee from the dawn of the day.

My soul hath thirsted after thee, *oh, by how many titles doth my whole being belong to thee!

In this desert, uncultivated and barren land, *I shall be in thy presence, as if I were in the sanctuary, to contemplate thy power and thy glory.

For thy mercies are preferable to many lives, *my lips shall not cease to praise thee.

Thus I will bless thee all my life, *and I will lift up my hands to praise thy name.

May my soul be replenished with thy benedictions, as with the fatness of marrow, *and my mouth shall praise thee with rapturous joy.

I have called thee to mynd on my bed at night, and in the morning I will meditate on thee, *because thou hast been my helper.

Under the covert of thy wings I will rejoice, my soul is attached to thee, *thy right hand hath protected me.

And my enemies have in vain sought my soul, they shall descend into the lower regions of the earth, *unto the justice of the sword they shall be delivered, and shall become a prey to ravenous foxes.

But the king shall rejoice in God. All who swear by him shall be glorified, *because he hath stopped the mouths of those who speak evil things.

The Versicle, Eternal Rest, is not said here.

Psalm 67

May God have mercy on us and bless us, *may he regard us with a favorable countenance and have mercy on us.

May we know thy ways on earth, *and may all nations seek thy salvation.

May the people confess to thee, O God, *may all present to thee their praises.

Let the nations be glad and rejoice, *for thou dost judge the people with equity, and rulest over all the nations of the earth.

May the people confess to thee, O God, may all present to thee their praises, *the earth hath yielded forth her fruit.

May the Lord our God bless us, may he give us his blessing, *and may all the bounds of the earth fear him.

Eternal rest grant to them, O Lord, *And may perpetual light shine upon them.

Anthem. Thy right hand, O Lord, hath supported me.

Anthem
From the gates of hell deliver their souls, O Lord.

Canticle of Ezekiel
Isaiah 38
I said within myself, Shall I in the midst of my days, *go down to the grave?

In vain have I expected the residue of my years, *alas! I said, I shall not see my Lord God in the land of the living.

I shall not see man anymore, *dwelling in peaceful security.

My generation is at an end and is broken up, *like the tents of shepherds.

My life is suddenly cut off, like a weaver cuts the warp, so am I taken away, *thou wilt finish my life in the course of a day, between the morning and the evening.

I did hope to live till morning, *but my illness, like a furious lion, hath broken my frame to pieces.

Thou wilt finish my life in the course of a day, between the morning and evening, *I will mourn then like a young swallow, I will sigh from my heart like a dove.

My eyes are become weak *by looking up constantly towards heaven.

O Lord, I suffer much, do thou answer for me, *What shall I say, or what will he reply to me, whereas he himself hath done it?

I will recollect and recount to thee all the years of my life, *in the bitterness of my soul.

O Lord, if such be the life of man, and if my life be occupied in such things, thou wilt chastise me, and preserve my soul, *for behold, to be without correction is the most deplorable of all afflictions.

Thou hast at length rescued my soul from perdition, *and hast cancelled and buried in oblivion all my sins.

For those in hell shall not bless thee, nor shall the dead sing forth thy praises, *those who are condemned to the burning lake shall not receive thy salvation.

The living, O Lord, the living people shall praise thee as I do this day, *the fathers shall declare to their children thy promised salvation.

O Lord, save my soul, *and we shall sing canticles to thee all the days of our lives in the temple of the Lord.

Eternal rest grant to them, O Lord, *And may perpetual light shine upon them.

Anthem. From the gates of hell deliver their souls, O Lord.

Anthem

Let every living creature praise the Lord.

Psalm 148

Praise the Lord in the heavens, *praise him in the highest places.

Praise him all ye his angels, *praise him ye celestial powers.

Praise him sun and moon, *praise him all ye stars and light.

Praise him O heaven of heavens! *And may the waters that are over the firmament praise the name of the Lord.

For he hath spoken the word, and all things were made, *he hath commanded and they were created.

He hath established his works for length of ages, *he prescribed to them his wise regulations which shall not be transgressed.

Praise the Lord from the earth, *ye dragons and all ye depths.

Fire, hail, snow, ice, and stormy winds, *which obey his orders.

Mountains and all hills, *fruit bearing trees and all cedars.

Beasts and herds of cattle, *reptiles and birds of the air.

Kings of the earth and all ye people, *princes and judges of the earth.

Young men and maidens, the old with the young, let them praise the name of the Lord, *for his name alone is most worthy of all praise.

His praise is above heaven and earth, *and he hath exalted the power of his people.

May hymns of praise be rendered to him by all his saints, *by the children of Israel, his cherished people.

The Versicle, Eternal Rest, *is not said here.*

Psalm 149

Sing to the Lord a new canticle, *may his praises resound in the assembly of the saints.

May Israel rejoice in the God who made him, *may the sons of Sion exult in their king.

May they celebrate his name in choir, *and honor him by concert on the timbrel and psaltery.

For the Lord is well pleased with his people, *and he will exalt the meek unto salvation.

The saints in glory shall be filled with joy, *they shall rejoice on their couches.

Sublime praises of God are in their mouths, *and two edged swords in their hands.

To execute vengeance on the nations, *and chastisement on the people.

To bind their kings in fetters, *and their nobles with iron

manacles.

They shall thus exercise the decreed justice, *this glory is reserved for all his saints.

The Versicle, Eternal Rest, *is not said here.*

Psalm 150

Praise the Lord in his sanctuary, *praise him in the firmament of his power.

Praise him in his mighty deeds, *praise him according to his exceeding greatness.

Praise him on the timbrel and in choir, *praise him on the psaltery and the harp.

Praise him with the best sounding cymbals, praise him on instruments of jubilee. *May every living creature praise the Lord.

Eternal rest grant to them, O Lord, *And may perpetual light shine upon them.

Anthem. Let every living creature praise the Lord.

V. I have heard a voice from heaven saying to me,

R. Blessed are the dead who repose in the Lord.

Anthem

I am the resurrection and the life. He who believeth in me, although he were dead, shall live; and every one who liveth and believeth in me shall not meet with eternal death.

Canticle of Zechariah
Luke 1: 68

Blessed be the Lord, the God of Israel, *because he hath visited and effected the redemption of his people.

And he hath raised up a powerful Savior for us, *in the house of David his servant.

As he promised by the mouth of his holy prophets, *from the beginning.

To save us from our enemies, *and from the hands of all who hate us.

To communicate his mercy to us, as well as to our fathers, *and to recall to mind the holy covenant made to them.

The oath, which he hath sworn to our father Abraham, *that

he would grant us the grace,

That, being rescued from the fear and power of our enemies, *we may serve him,

In holiness and righteousness in his presence, *all the days of our lives.

And thou, O happy child, *shalt be called the prophet of the Most High, *for thou shalt go before the face of the Lord to prepare his ways.

To give his people the knowledge of salvation, *unto the remission of their sins.

Through the bowels of the mercy of our God, *with which he like the rising sun from on high hath visited us.

To give light to those who sit in darkness and in the shadow of death, *to guide our feet into the ways of peace.

Eternal rest grant to them, O Lord, *And may perpetual light shine upon them.

Anthem. I am the resurrection and the life. He who believeth in me, although he were dead shall live, and everyone who liveth and believeth in me shall not meet with eternal death.

The following prayers and Versicles are said for one deceased person only. The prayers for many deceased persons are below, and the prayers for the deceased in general (when the office is of a simple rite) follow those.
Note: These prayers are also said after the Anthem of the Canticle of the Blessed Virgin Mary at Vespers.

Our Father, _in silence._

V. And lead us not into temptation.

R. But deliver us from evil.

V. From the gates of hell.

R. Deliver his (her) soul, O Lord

V. May he (she) rest in peace.

R. Amen

V. O Lord, hear my prayer.

R. And let my cry come unto thee.

V. The Lord be with thee.

The following verse is omitted by the presider if he is not a priest or deacon.

R. _And with thy Spirit._

Various Prayers for the Dead

Prayer on the day of death or burial

Absolve, we beseech thee O Lord, the soul of thy servant, N. that being dead to this world, he (she) may live to thee, and that he (she) may obtain from thy great mercy the plenary remission of his (her) sins, committed by human frailty while on earth. Through our Lord Jesus Christ, thy Son, who liveth and reigneth with thee and the Holy Ghost, one God, world without end.

R. Amen.

Another prayer on the day of death or burial

O God, whose attribute is always to have mercy and to spare, we humbly present our prayers to thee for the soul of thy servant N., which thou hast this day called out of this world, beseeching thee not to deliver it into the hands of the enemy, nor to forget it forever, but to command thy holy angels to receive it, and to bear it into paradise, that as it has believed and hoped in thee, it may be delivered from the pains of hell, and inherit eternal life. Through our Lord Jesus Christ, thy Son, who liveth and reigneth with thee and the Holy Ghost, one God, world without end.

R. Amen.

Prayer on the third, seventh, or thirtieth day after death

Admit, we beseech thee, O Lord, the soul of thy servant N. on this the third (or seventh, or thirtieth) day of death, which we commemorate, into the society of thy saints, and refresh it with the perpetual dew of thy mercy. Through our Lord Jesus Christ, thy Son, who liveth and reigneth with thee and the Holy Ghost, one God, world without end.

R. Amen.

Prayer on the anniversary day of death

O God, the Lord of mercy, grant to the soul of thy servant N. whose anniversary day of death we commemorate, a place of comfort, a happy rest, and the light of glory. Through our Lord

Jesus Christ, thy Son, who liveth and reigneth with thee and the Holy Ghost, one God, world without end.

R. Amen.

Other Different Prayers for the Dead

Prayer for the Sovereign Pontiff, deceased

O God, who wast pleased in thy divine providence to have thy servant N. numbered among the chief pastors of thy Church, grand we beseech thee, that he who represented the person of thy only begotten Son on earth, may be admitted into the company of the holy prelates in heaven. Through the same Lord Jesus Christ thy Son, who liveth and reigneth with thee and the Holy Ghost, one God, world without end.

R. Amen

Prayer for a deceased Bishop or Priest

O God, by whose favor thy servant N. was raised to the dignity of a bishop (priest), and honored with the apostolic functions, grant we beseech thee, he may be admitted into the eternal society of thy apostles in heaven. Through our Lord Jesus Christ, thy Son, who liveth and reigneth with thee and the Holy Ghost, one God, world without end.

R. Amen

Another prayer for a deceased Bishop

Hear our prayer, O Lord, and grant that the soul of thy servant and bishop N. whom thou hast rescued from the painful conflicts of this world, may partake of the bliss of thy saints. Through our Lord Jesus Christ thy Son, who liveth and reigneth with thee and the Holy Ghost, one God, world without end.

R. Amen.

Another prayer for a deceased Priest

Grant, we beseech thee, O Lord, that the soul of thy servant N. whom thou hast adorned with the sacred character of priesthood whilst on earth, may forever rejoice in celestial bliss. Through our Lord Jesus Christ thy Son, who liveth and reigneth with thee and the Holy Ghost, one God, world without end.

R. Amen.

Prayer for a deceased Father or Mother

O God, who hast commanded us to honor our father and mother, mercifully show pity to the soul of my father (mother), forgive his faults (her faults), and grant that I may see him (her) hereafter in the joys of thy eternal glory. Through our Lord Jesus Christ thy Son, who liveth and reigneth with thee and the Holy Ghost, one God, world without end.

R. Amen.

Prayer for a Man deceased

Graciously hear, O Lord, the prayers we address to thee, by which we humbly entreat thy mercy to receive into the kingdom of peace and light, the soul of thy servant N. whom thou hast called out of this world, and to reckon him among the blessed. Through our Lord Jesus Christ thy Son, who liveth and reigneth with thee and the Holy Ghost, one God, world without end.

R. Amen.

Prayer for a Woman deceased

We beseech thee, O Lord, to show thy bountiful mercy to the soul of thy servant N. and being now freed from the corruption of this mortal life, grant to her the portion of thy eternal inheritance of bliss. Through our Lord Jesus Christ thy Son, who liveth and reigneth with thee and the Holy Ghost, one God, world without end.

R. Amen.

After the proper Prayer, the following Versicles are said in the plural number, although the office and prayer be for only one deceased.

V. Eternal rest grant to them, O Lord.
R. And may perpetual light shine upon them.
V. May they rest in peace.
R. Amen.

The following Prayers are said for many deceased Persons: after the Anthem of the Canticle, as above, is said the Lord's Prayer, etc.

Our Father, *in silence.*
V. And lead us not into temptation
R. But deliver us from evil.
V. From the gates of hell.
R. Deliver their souls, O Lord.
V. May they rest in peace.
R. Amen
V. O Lord, hear my prayer.
R. And let my cry come unto thee.

If a Priest or Deacon officiates, he adds:

V. The Lord be with you.
R. And with thy Spirit.

Prayer on the Commemoration of All Souls
O God, the creator and redeemer of all the faithful, give to the souls of thy servants departed the full remission of all their sins, that through the help of pious supplications they may obtain the pardon they have always desired. Who livest and reignest with the Father and the Holy Ghost, one God, world without end. Amen.

Prayer on the anniversary of many deceased persons
O God, the Lord of mercy, grant to the souls of thy servants, whose anniversary day of decease we commemorate, a place of comfort, a happy rest, and the light of glory. Through our Lord Jesus Christ thy Son, who liveth and reigneth with thee and the Holy Ghost, one God, world without end.
R. Amen.

Prayer for many Bishops and Priests deceased
O God, by whose favor thy servants were raised to the dignity of bishops and priests, grant we beseech thee, that they may be admitted into the eternal society of thy apostles in heaven. Through our Lord Jesus Christ thy Son, who liveth and reigneth with thee and the Holy Ghost, one God, world without end.
R. Amen

Prayer for both Father and Mother deceased

O God, who hast commanded us to honor our father and mother (our fathers and mothers), mercifully show pity to the souls of my (our) parents, forgive them their faults, and grant me (us) the grace to see them hereafter in the joys of eternal glory. Through our Lord Jesus Christ thy Son, who liveth and reigneth with thee and the Holy Ghost, one God, world without end.

Prayer for deceased brethren, relations, and benefactors

O God, bounteous in mercy, and lover of the salvation of mankind, we humbly beseech thy divine clemency to grant to the brethren of our holy society, and to our relations and benefactors who are departed fro this life, through the intercession of the ever blessed Virgin Mary, and of all the saints, thou wouldst receive them into their company in the fruition of eternal bliss. Through our Lord Jesus Christ thy Son, who liveth and reigneth with thee and the Holy Ghost, one God, world without end.

R. Amen.

After the proper prayer are said the following Versicles

V. Eternal rest grant to them, O Lord.

R. And let perpetual light shine upon them.

V. May they rest in peace.

R. Amen.

When the office is said through devotion in any other time of the year, and when it is daily recited for the souls departed in general, the Invitatory is omitted, one Nocturn only is said, according to the day, and the first words only of the Anthems are said before the Psalms, like the feast of a simple rite. After the Anthem of the Canticle the following prayers, Psalm, and Versicles, are always recited *kneeling:*

Our Father, *in silence.*

V. And lead us not into temptation.

R. But deliver us from evil.

Then the following Psalm is said at Lauds, but at Vespers in its stead is recited the Psalm, Praise the Lord, as below:

Psalm 130

From the depths I have cried out to thee, *O gracious Lord hear my voice.

Let thy ears be attentive *to the voice of my petition.

If thou wilt consider our iniquities, O mighty Lord, *who shall endure it?

But with thee there is merciful forgiveness, *and by reason of thy law, I have waited for thee, O Lord.

My soul hath relied on his word, *my soul hath hoped in the Lord.

From the morning watch even until night, *let Israel hope in the Lord.

Because with the Lord there is mercy, *and with him plentiful redemption.

And he shall redeem Israel *from all his iniquities.

Eternal rest grant to them, O Lord, *And may perpetual light shine upon them.

At the end of Vespers, instead of the Psalm From the Depths, the following is said:

Psalm 146

Praise the Lord, O my soul, I will give praises to him all my life, *I will sing canticles to my God as long as I exist.

Place not your trust in princes, *nor in the children of men, who cannot save you.

The soul shall quit the body, which shall return to its mother earth, *on that fatal day all their designs shall vanish.

Blessed is he who hath the God of Jacob for his helper, whose hope is in the Lord his God, *who made heaven and earth, the sea, and all that they contain.

Who keepeth his promise forever and doth justice to those who are oppressed, *who giveth food to the hungry.

The Lord looseth the captives' chains, *the Lord giveth sight to the blind.

The Lord raiseth up those who are cast down, *the Lord loveth the righteous.

The Lord is the guardian of strangers, he will protect the orphan and the widow, *but the ways of sinners he will destroy.

The Lord shall reign forever, he is thy God, O Sion, *unto all generations.

Eternal rest grant to them, O Lord, *And may perpetual light shine upon them.

After the respective Psalms, are said the following Versicles:

V. From the gates of hell.

R. Deliver their souls, O Lord.

V. May they rest in peace.

R. Amen.

V. O Lord, hear my prayer.

R. And let my cry come unto thee.

If the presider is a priest or deacon, he adds:

V. The Lord be with you.

R. And with thy Spirit.

Let us pray

O God, by whose favor thy servants were raised to the dignity of bishops and priests, grant we beseech thee, that they may be admitted into the eternal society of thy apostles in heaven.

O God, bounteous in mercy, and lover of the salvation of mankind, we humbly beseech thy divine clemency in behalf of the brethren of our holy society, our relations and benefactors, who are departed from this life, through the intercession of the ever blessed Virgin Mary and of all the saints, that thou wouldst receive them into their company in the fruition of eternal bliss. Through our Lord Jesus Christ who liveth and reigneth with thee and the Holy Ghost, one God, world without end.

O God, the creator and redeemer of all the faithful, give to the souls of thy servants departed the full remission of all their sins, that through the help of pious supplications they may obtain the pardon they have always desired. Who livest and reignest, world without end.

R. Amen.

V. Eternal rest grant to them, O Lord.

R. And let perpetual light shine upon them.
V. May they rest in peace.
R. Amen.

The Following Sequence

Is said at Mass for the Dead, and may be recited through devotion after the Office for the Dead:

The day of wrath, most dreadful day,
The world in ashes waste shall lay,
As David and the Sibyls say.
What horror shall invade the mind,
When Christ, the judge of all mankind,
Our grievous cromes will clearly find!
The trumpets shall send forth their sound,
Which will through monuments rebound,
To rouse the dead from underground.
Both death and nature with surprise
Shall see each creature quickly rise,
To view the Judge with their own eyes.
Then shall, with universal dread,
The great accounting book be read,
To try the living and the dead.
The Judge will mount his awful throne,
And make all secret sins be known:
Each convict shall confess his own.
Wretched me! What shall I say?
What advocate will make my plea?
The just will scarce be saved that day.
O mighty and tremendous King!
Of grace the author, source, and spring,
To us thy saving mercy bring.
O Jesus dear, forget not me.
Who caused thy painful agony,
Condemn me not eternally.
My soul has cost thee too much pain:
Thy precious blood the cross did stain:
Let not thy ransom be in vain.

Just Judge, whom all the powers obey,
Forgive my debt, too great to pay,
Before the dread accounting day.
I sigh, I groan, I'm seized with fears,
A load of sin my conscience bears:
O God, vouchsafe, accept my tears.
Thou didst receive Magdalen's grief;
Thou didst absolve the convert thief;
This gives me hope of sure relief.
Do not reject my mournful prayer;
Release me from that sinful snare,
For which a hell thou didst prepare.
Among thy sheep give me a place;
Drive far the goats, the' infernal race:
Elect me as thy heir of grace.
From that most dismal deep abyss,
Where flames devour and serpents hiss,
Promote me to thy seats of bliss.
Prostrate, my contrite heart I rend;
I bow my head, my knees I bend;
On that last day be thou my friend.
Thrice sad and bitter day for those,
Who stained with sin did their life close.
Their doom shall be eternal woes.
On those, who living did their best,
Bestow, O Lord, eternal rest.
And grant them glory with the blest.
Amen.

Exequies, or Sacred Rites Over the Tomb

Solemnity performed after High Mass for the Dead, and which may be privately recited after the office:

Responsory

Deliver me, O Lord, from eternal death on that dreadful day, *When the heavens and earth shall be moved: *Whilst thou wilt come to judge the world by fire.

V. I am seized with trembling and dread, when I reflect on

the rigorous examination and the vengeful wrath of that day.

R. When the heavens and earth shall be moved.

V. That day shall be a day of wrath, calamity, and misery: the great day of extreme bitterness and terror.

R. Whilst thou wilt come to judge the world by fire.

V. Eternal rest grant to them, O Lord, and may perpetual light shine upon them.

R. Deliver me, O Lord, from eternal death on that dreadful day, when the heavens and earth shall be moved, whilst thou wilt come to judge the world by fire.

Lord, have mercy on us.

Christ, have mercy on us.

Lord, have mercy on us.

Our Father, *in silence.*

V. And lead us not into temptation.

R. But deliver us from evil.

V. From the gates of hell.

R. Deliver his soul (their souls), O Lord.

V. May he (they) rest in peace.

R. Amen

V. O Lord, hear my prayer.

R. And let my cry come unto thee.

Let us pray

The proper Prayer for one or more deceased, is one of the above Prayers at the end of Lauds, but with the short conclusion, Through Christ our Lord. R. Amen.

Psalm 130

From the depths I have cried out to thee, *O gracious Lord hear my voice.

Let thy ears be attentive *to the voice of my petition.

If thou wilt consider our iniquities, O mighty Lord, *who shall endure it?

But with thee there is merciful forgiveness, *and by reason of thy law, I have waited for thee, O Lord.

My soul hath relied on his word, *my soul hath hoped in the Lord.

From the morning watch even until night, *let Israel hope in the Lord.

Because with the Lord there is mercy, *and with him plentiful redemption.

And he shall redeem Israel *from all his iniquities.

Eternal rest grant to them, O Lord, *And may perpetual light shine upon them.

Lord, have mercy on us.

Christ, have mercy on us.

Lord, have mercy on us.

Our Father, *in silence.*

V. And lead us not into temptation.

R. But deliver us from evil.

V. From the gates of hell.

R. Deliver his soul (their souls), O Lord.

V. May he (they) rest in peace.

R. Amen

V. O Lord, hear my prayer.

R. And let my cry come unto thee.

Let us pray

O God, the Creator and redeemer of all the faithful, give to the souls of thy servants departed, the full remission of all their sins: that through the help of pious supplication, they may obtain the pardon they have always desired: Who livest and reignest world without end.

R. Amen.

V. Eternal rest grant to them, O Lord.

R. And may perpetual light shine upon them.

V. May they rest in peace.

R. Amen.

V. May his soul (their souls), and may the souls of all the faithful departed, through the mercy of God, rest in peace.

R. Amen.

The Prayers after the Office may be said.
End of the Office for the Dead

Various Other Prayers

Anthem

Under thy protection we seek refuge, O holy mother of God;
despise not our petitions in our necessities, but deliver us
continually from all dangers, O glorious and blessed Virgin

The Litany of Loreto

Lord, have mercy upon us.
Christ, have mercy upon us.
Lord have mercy upon us
Christ hear us
Christ, graciously hear us.
God, the Father of Heaven,
Have mercy upon us.
God, the Son, Redeemer of the world
Have mercy upon us.
God, the Holy Ghost,
Have mercy upon us.
Holy Trinity, one God,
Have mercy upon us.
Holy Mary,   *pray for us!*
Holy Mother of God,
Holy Virgin of Virgins
Mother of Christ,
Mother of divine grace,
Mother most pure,
Mother most chaste,
Mother undefiled,
Mother inviolate,
Mother most amiable,
Mother most admirable,
Mother of our Creator,
Mother of our Redeemer,
Virgin most prudent,
Virgin most venerable,
Virgin most renowned,
Virgin post powerful,

Virgin most merciful,
Virgin most faithful,
Mirror of justice,
Seat of wisdom,
Cause of our joy,
Spiritual vessel,
Vessel of honor,
Vessel of singular devotion,
Mystical Rose,
Tower of David,
Tower of ivory,
House of gold,
Ark of the covenant,
Gate of heaven,
Morning star,
Health of the weak,
Refuge of sinners,
Comfortress of the afflicted,
Help of Christians,
Queen of angels,
Queen of patriarchs,
Queen of prophets,
Queen of apostles,
Queen of martyrs,
Queen of confessors,
Queen of virgins,
Queen of all saints,
Lamb of God, who takest away the sins of the world,
Spare us, O Lord
Lamb of God, who takest away the sins of the world,
Hear us, O Lord.
Lamb of God, who takest away the sins of the world,
Have mercy upon us.
Anthem. Under thy protection we seek refuge, O holy mother of God; despise not our petitions in our necessities, but deliver us continually from all dangers, O glorious and blessed Virgin
V. Pray for us, O holy Mother of God.
R. That we may be made worthy of the promises of Christ.

Let us pray

Pour forth, we beseech thee, O Lord, thy diving grace into our hearts, that we to whom the incarnation of Christ thy Son was made known by the message of an angel, may by his passion and cross be brought to the glory of his resurrection, through the same Christ our Lord. Amen.

The Acts

A Prayer before the Acts

O Almighty and eternal God! Grant unto us an increase in Faith, Hope, and Charity; and that we may obtain what thou hast promised, make us love and practice what thou commandest, through Jesus Christ our Lord. Amen.

An Act of Contrition

O my God! I am heartily sorry for having offended thee, and I detest my sins most sincerely, because they displease thee, my God, who art so deserving of all my love, for thy infinite goodness and most admirable perfections, and I firmly purpose, by thy holy grace, never more to offend thee.

An Act of Faith

O my God! I firmly believe that thou art one only God, the Creator and Sovereign Lord of Heaven and Earth, infinitely great and infinitely good. I firmly believe that in thee, one only God, there are three Divine Persons, really distinct and equal in all things, the Father, the Son, and the Holy Ghost. I firmly believe, that Jesus Christ, God the Son, became Man, that he was conceived by the Holy Ghost, and was born of the Virgin Mary, that he suffered and died on a cross to redeem and save us, that he arose the third day from the dead, that he ascended into heaven, that he will come at the end of the world to judge mankind, and that he will reward the good with eternal happiness, and condemn the wicked to the everlasting pains of hell. I believe these, and all other articles which the holy Roman Catholic Church proposes to our belief, because thou, my God, the Infallible Truth, hast revealed them, and thou hast commanded us to hear the Church, which is the pillar and ground of truth. In this faith I am firmly resolved, by thy holy grace, to live and die.

An Act of Hope

O my God, who hast graciously promised every blessing, even heaven itself, through Jesus Christ, to those who keep thy commandments, relying on thy infinite power, goodness, and mercy, and confiding in thy sacred promises, to which thou art always faithful, I confidently hope to obtain pardon of all my sins, grace to serve thee faithfully in this life, and eternal happiness in the next, through my Lord and Savior Jesus Christ.

An Act of Charity

O my God! I love thee with my whole heart and soul, and above all things, because thou art infinitely good and perfect, and most worthy of all my love, and for thy sake I love my neighbor as myself. Mercifully grant, O my God! That having loved thee on earth, I may love and enjoy thee forever in heaven. Amen.

Litany of the Holy Name of Jesus

Lord, have mercy on us.
Christ, have mercy on us.
Lord, have mercy on us
Christ hear us
Christ graciously hear us.
God, the Father of Heaven,   **have mercy on us.**
God, the Son, Redeemer of the world,
God, the Holy Ghost,
Holy Trinity, one God,
Jesus, Son of the living God,
Jesus, Splendor of the Father,
Jesus, Brightness of eternal light,
Jesus, King of glory,
Jesus, Sun of justice,
Jesus, Son of the Virgin Mary,
Jesus, most amiable,
Jesus, most adorable,
Jesus, the mighty God,
Jesus, Father of the World to come,
Jesus, Angel of the Great Council,
Jesus, most powerful,

Jesus, most patient,
Jesus, most obedient,
Jesus, meek and humble of heart,
Jesus, lover of chastity,
Jesus, lover of peace,
Jesus lover uf us,
Jesus, author of life,
Jesus, example of virtues,
Jesus, zealous lover of souls,
Jesus, our God,
Jesus, our refuge,
Jesus, father of the poor,
Jesus, treasure of the faithful,
Jesus, good Shepherd,
Jesus, true light,
Jesus, eternal wisdom,
Jesus, infinite goodness,
Jesus, the Way, the Truth, and the Life,
Jesus, joy of angels,
Jesus, King of patriarchs,
Jesus, inspirer of the prophets,
Jesus, Master of the Apostles,
Jesus, teacher of the Evangelists,
Jesus, strength of martyrs,
Jesus, light of confessors,
Jesus, spouse of virgins,
Jesus, crown of all Saints,
Be merciful unto us, *Spare us O Lord Jesus!*
Be merciful unto us, *Hear us, O Lord Jesus!*
From all sin, *Lord Jesus, deliver us.*
From thy wrath,
From the snares of the devil,
From the spirit of uncleanness,
From everlasting death,
From the neglect of thy holy inspirations,
Through the mystery of thy holy incarnation,
Through thy nativity,
Through thy divine infancy,
Through thy sacred life,
Through thy labors,

Through thy cross and passion,
Through thy pain and torments,
Through thy death and burial,
Through thy glorious resurrection,
Through thy triumphant ascension,
Through thy joys and glory,
In the day of judgment,
Lamb of God, who takest away the sins of the world,
Spare us, O Lord Jesus!
Lamb of God, who takest away the sins of the world,
Hear us, O Lord Jesus!
*Lam*b of God, who takest away the sins of the world,
Have mercy on us, O Lord Jesus!
Lord Jesus, hear us!
Lord Jesus, graciously hear us!

Let us pray

O Lord Jesus Christ, who hast said, Ask and ye shall receive, seek and ye shall find, knock and it shall be opened unto you, mercifully attend to our supplications, and grand us the gift of divine charity, that we may ever love thee with our whole hearts, and never cease from praising thy holy name, who livest and reigneth one God, world without end. Amen.

Litany for a Happy Death

O Lord Jesus, God of goodness and Father of mercies, I approach thee with a contrite and humble heart, to thee I recommend the last hour of my life, and the decision of my eternal doom.

When my feet, benumbed with death, shall admonish me that my mortal course is drawing to an end, *merciful Jesus, have mercy on me.*

When my eyes, dim and troubled at the approach of death, shall fix themselves on thee, my last and only support, *merciful Jesus, have mercy on me.*

When my face, pale and livid, shall inspire the beholders with pity and dismay; when my hair, bathed in the sweat of death and stiffening on my head shall forbode my approaching end, *merciful Jesus, have mercy on me.*

When my ears, soon to be forever shut to the discourse of creatures, shall be open to the irrevocable decree which is to cut me off from the number of the living, *merciful Jesus, have mercy on me.*

When my imagination, agitated by dreadful specters, shall be sunk in an abyss of anguish; when my soul, affrightened with the sight of my iniquities and the terrors of thy judgment, shall have to fight against the angel of darkness, who will endeavor to conceal thy mercies from my eyes, and to plunge me into despair, *merciful Jesus, have mercy on me.*

When my poor heart, yielding to the pressures and exhausted by its frequent struggles against the enemies of its salvation, shall feel the pangs of death, *merciful Jesus, have mercy on me.*

When the last tear, the forerunner of my dissolution, shall drop from my eyes, receive it as a sacrifice of expiation from my sins; grant that I may expire the victim of penance and in that dreadful moment, *merciful Jesus, have mercy on me.*

When my friends, encircling my bed, shall shed the tears of pity over me, and invoke thy clemency in my behalf, *merciful Jesus, have mercy on me.*

When I shall have lost the use of my senses; when the world shall have vanished from my sight; when my agonizing soul shall feel the sorrows of death, *merciful Jesus, have mercy on me.*

When my last sigh shall summon my soul to burst from the embraces of the body, and to spring to thee on the wings of impatience and desire, *merciful Jesus, have mercy on me.*

When my soul, trembling on my lips, shall bid adieu to the world and leave my body lifeless, pale, and cold, receive this separation as an homage, which I willingly pay to thy Divine Majesty, and in that last moment of my mortal life, *merciful Jesus, have mercy on me.*

When at length my soul, admitted to thy presence shall first behold the splendor of thy majesty, reject me not, but receive me into thy bosom, where I may forever sing thy praises, and in that moment, when eternity shall begin to me, *merciful Jesus, have mercy on me.*

Let us pray

O God, who hast doomed all to die, but hast concealed from all their hour of their death, grant that I may pass my days in the practice of thy holiness and justice; and that I may deserve to quit

this world in the peace of a good conscience, and in the
embraces of thy love, through Christ our Lord. Amen.
Lord have mercy on us.
Lord have mercy on us.
Christ have mercy on us.
Christ have mercy on us.
Lord have mercy on us.
Lord have mercy on us.
Jesus, receive our prayers.
Lord Jesus, grant our petitions.

O God the Father, Creator of the world,
Have mercy on the souls of the faithful departed.
O God the Son, Redeemer of mankind,
Deliver the souls of the faithful departed,
O God the Holy Ghost, perfector of the elect,
Accomplish the bliss of the faithful departed.
　　Blessed Virgin Mary, who, by the special privilege of grace,
wast triumphantly assumed into the Kingdom of Thy Son,
Pray for the souls of the faithful departed. *
Blessed Angels, who, ordering aright the first act of your will,
were fixed forthwith in unchangeable happiness, *
Blessed Patriarchs, who were filled with joy when the Desired of
Nations put an end to your captivity, *
Blessed Prophets, who, after patiently awaiting the arrival of the
Messiah, were at length consoled by a visit from Him in person,
*
Blessed Saints, who, at the glorious Resurrection of Our Savior,
were translated from Limbo to the visible Presence of God, *
Blessed Apostles, who at the last day shall sit to judge the twelve
tribes of Israel, *
Blessed Disciples of Our Lord, who followed His steps in the
paths of perfection, *
Blessed Martyrs, who passed through the sea of your own blood,
entering immediately into the Land of Promise, *
Blessed Confessors, who despised the vanity of the earth, and
placed your affections on the joys of heaven, *
Blessed Virgins, who, with your lighted lamps, awaited the
coming of the heavenly Spouse, *
O Holy Saints, who, being freed from all irregular attachment to

creatures, were perfectly fitted for immediate union with your Creator, *

Be merciful, O Lord, and pardon their sins.

Be merciful, O Lord, and hear their prayers.

From the shades of death, where the light of Thy countenance shineth not,

Deliver them, O Lord. **

From the evils to which immortification in this world must expose them in the other, **

From Thy displeasure, provoked by negligence and ingratitude, **

From the pains of purgatory, so justly inflicted upon unexpiated sins, **

From the torments incomparably greater than the bitterest anguish of this life, **

By the multitude of Thy mercies, ever compassionate to human frailties, **

By the virtue of Thy Cross, whereon Thou reconciled the world to Thy Father, **

By Thy victorious descent into hell, to break the chains of death, **

By Thy glorious Resurrection from the tomb, to open the Kingdom of Heaven, **

By Thy triumphant Ascension into heaven, to lead captivity captive, **

By Thy dread coming to judge the world, **

We sinners: Beseech Thee to hear us.

That it please Thee to hasten the day when Thy faithful shall be delivered from the mansions of sorrow,

We beseech Thee to hear us. ***

That it please Thee to shorten the time of their expiation, and to admit them speedily into Thy heavenly sanctuary, ***

That it please Thee, through the prayers and good works performed in Thy Church, to receive them into Thy eternal tabernacles, ***

That it please Thee to accept, in atonement for their sins, the infinite value of Thy unbloody Sacrifice, ***

That the blessed view of Jesus may comfort them, and His unfading glory shine upon them, ***

That the whole Church Triumphant may soon celebrate their deliverance; and the choirs of angels sing new hymns of Joy, on their never ending happiness, ***
That we ourselves may share in their triumph, and unite with all the citizens of heaven in eternal alleluias, ***
Son of God: We beseech Thee to hear us.

Lamb of God, Who shalt come with glory to judge the living and the dead:
Give rest to the souls of the faithful departed.
Lamb of God, at Whose Presence the heavens and the earth shall be moved:
Give rest to the souls of the faithful departed.

Lamb of God, in Whose book of life the names of Thy elect are inscribed:
Give rest to the souls of the faithful departed.

Anthem: Deliver us, O Lord, from eternal death, in that tremendous day when the heavens and the earth shall be moved, whilst Thou shalt come to judge the world by fire. We tremble and are sore afraid at the discussion which shall take place, and at Thy future wrath, when the heavens shall be moved, and the earth, when Thou shalt come to judge the world by fire. That day is a day of wrath, of calamity, of misery, a great and most bitter day, when Thou shalt come to judge the world by fire.
V. Give them, O Lord, eternal rest:
R. And let perpetual light shine upon them. Amen.

Let us pray

Grant to Thy servants departed, O Lord, we beseech Thee, Thy mercy, that they who prayed that Thy will be done, may not receive punishments for their misdeeds but that, even as here below the true faith united them to the ranks of the faithful, so in heaven by Thy mercy they may have fellowship with the choirs of angels. Through Christ Our Lord.

R. Amen.

Litany of the Saints

Lord, have mercy on us.
Lord have mercy on us.
Christ, have mercy on us.
Christ have mercy on us.
Lord, have mercy on us.
Lord, have mercy on us.
Christ, hear us.
Christ, hear us.
Christ, graciously hear us.
Christ, graciously hear us.
God the Father of heaven,
Have mercy on us.
God the Son, Redeemer of the world,
Have mercy on us
God the Holy Ghost,
Have mercy on us
Holy Trinity, one God,
Have mercy on us
Holy Mary,   ...**pray for us**
Holy Mother of God,
Holy Virgin of virgins,
St. Michael,
St. Gabriel,
St. Raphael,
All ye holy Angels and Archangels,
All ye holy orders of blessed Spirits,
St. John the Baptist,
St. Joseph,
All ye holy Patriarchs and Prophets,
St. Peter,
St. Paul,
St. Andrew,
St. James,
St. John,
St. Thomas,
St. James,
St. Philip,
St. Bartholomew,
St. Matthew,

St. Simon,
St. Thaddeus,
St. Matthias,
St. Barnabas,
St. Luke,
St. Mark,
All ye holy Apostles and Evangelists,
All ye holy Disciples of the Lord,
All ye holy Innocents,
St. Stephen,
St. Lawrence,
St. Vincent,
SS. Fabian and Sebastian,
SS. John and Paul,
SS. Cosmas and Damian,
SS. Gervase and Protase,
All ye holy Martyrs,
St. Sylvester,
St. Gregory,
St. Ambrose,
St. Augustine,
St. Jerome,
St. Martin,
St. Nicholas,
All ye holy Bishops and Confessors,
All ye holy Doctors,
St. Anthony,
St. Benedict,
St. Bernard,
St. Dominic,
St. Francis,
All ye holy Priests and Levites,
All ye holy Monks and Hermits,
St. Mary Magdalen,
St. Agatha,
St. Lucy,
St. Agnes,
St. Cecilia,
St. Catherine,
St. Anastasia,

St. Brigid,
All ye holy Virgins and Widows,
All ye holy Saints of God,
Make intercession for us.
Be merciful to us,
Spare us, O Lord
Be merciful to us,
Graciously hear us, O Lord
From all evil,   **...O Lord deliver us!**
From all sin,
From Thy wrath,
From sudden and unlooked for death,
From the snares of the devil,
From anger, and hatred, and every evil will,
From the spirit of fornication,
From lightning and tempest,
From the scourge of earthquakes,
From plague, famine and war,
From everlasting death,
Through the mystery of Thy holy Incarnation,
Through Thy Coming,
Through Thy Birth,
Through Thy Baptism and holy Fasting,
Through Thy Cross and Passion,
Through Thy Death and Burial,
Through Thy holy Resurrection,
Through Thine admirable Ascension,
Through the coming of the Holy Ghost, the Comforter.
In the day of judgment,
 ...O Lord, We beseech thee to hear us.
We sinners,
That Thou wouldst spare us,
That Thou wouldst pardon us,
That Thou wouldst bring us to true penance,
That Thou wouldst vouchsafe to govern and preserve Thy holy Church,
That Thou wouldst vouchsafe to preserve our Apostolic Prelate, and all orders of the Church in holy religion,
That Thou wouldst vouchsafe to humble the enemies of holy Church,

That Thou wouldst vouchsafe to give peace and true concord to Christian kings and princes,

That Thou wouldst vouchsafe to grant peace and unity to the whole Christian world,

That Thou wouldst call back to the unity of the Church all who have strayed from her fold, and to guide all unbelievers into the light of the Gospel

That Thou wouldst vouchsafe to confirm and preserve us in Thy holy service,

That Thou wouldst lift up our minds to heavenly desires,

That Thou wouldst render eternal blessings to all our benefactors,

That Thou wouldst deliver our souls, and the souls of our brethren, relations, and benefactors, from eternal damnation,

That Thou wouldst vouchsafe to give and preserve the fruits of the earth,

That Thou wouldst vouchsafe to grant eternal rest to all the faithful departed,

That Thou wouldst vouchsafe graciously to hear us,

Lamb of God, who take away the sins of the world, *spare us, O Lord.*

Lamb of God, who take away the sins of the world, *graciously hear us, O Lord.*

Lamb of God, who take away the sins of the world, *have mercy on us.*

Christ, hear us.
Christ, graciously hear us.
Lord, have mercy,
Lord, have mercy.
Christ, have mercy,
Christ, have mercy.
Lord, have mercy,
Lord, have mercy.
Our Father *inaudibly*
V. And lead us not into temptation
R. But deliver us from evil. Amen.

Psalm 70

Incline unto mine aid, o God: O Lord, make haste to help me.

Let them be confounded and ashamed that seek my soul.

Let them forthwith be turned backward, and blush for shame, that desire evils to me.

Let them be turned backward, and blush, and be put to shame, who say to me, It is well! it is well!

Let all that seek thee be glad, and rejoice in thee: and let those who love thy salvation, say always, "our Lord be magnified."

But I am needy and poor! O God, help me. Thou art my helper and my deliverer, O Lord, make no delay.

V. (Profound bow) Glory be to the Father, and to the Son, and to the Holy Ghost

R. As it was in the beginning, is now, and ever shall be, world without end. Amen.

V. Save thy servants

R. Who put their trust in thee, my God.

V. Be to us, O Lord, a tower of strength

R. Against the face of the enemy

V. Let not the enemy prevail against us

R. Nor the son of iniquity have power to hurt us.

V. O Lord, deal not with us according to our sins

R. Nor reward us according to our iniquities.

V. Let us pray for our chief bishop N.

R. May the Lord preserve him, and prolong his life, and make him happy on earth, and deliver him not up to the will of his enemies.

V. Let us pray for our benefactors:

R. Vouchsafe, O Lord, for thy name's sake, to render eternal life to all those who do us good.

V. Let us pray for the faithful departed

R. Give them, O Lord, eternal rest: and let perpetual light shine unto them.

V. May they rest in peace.

R. Amen.

V. Save thy servants, O my God, who put their trust in thee.

V. Send them help, O Lord, from thy sanctuary

R. And from Sion protect them.

V. O Lord, hear my prayer

R. And let my supplication come unto thee.

Let us pray

O God, whose property it is always to have mercy and to spare, receive our petitions, that we and all thy servants, who are bound by the chain of sin, may, by the compassion of thy goodness, mercifully be absolved. Hear, we beseech thee, O Lord, the prayers of thy suppliants, and pardon our sins, who confess them to thee; that of thy bounty thou mayest grant us pardon and peace.

Out of thy clemency, O Lord, show us thy unspeakable mercy; that so thou mayest both acquit us of our sins, and deliver us from the punishment we deserve for them.

O God, who by sin art offended, and pacified by repentance, mercifully regard the prayers of thy people who make supplication to thee, and turn away the scourges of thy anger, which we deserve for our sins.

O Almighty and eternal God, have mercy on thy servant N. our chief Bishop, and direct him according to thy clemency, in the way of everlasting salvation, that by thy grace he may desire the things that are agreeable to thy will, and perform them with all his strength.

O God, from whom are all holy desires, righteous counsels, and just works, give to thy servants that peace which the world cannot give, that our hearts being disposed to keep thy commandments, and the fear of enemies taken away, the times, by thy protection, may be peaceable.

Inflame, O Lord, our reins and hearts with the fire of thy holy spirit, that we may serve thee with a chase body, and please thee with a clean heart.

O God, the Creator and Redeemer of all the faithful, give to the souls of thy servants departed the remission of all their sins, that by pious supplications they may obtain the pardon they have always desired.

Direct, we beseech thee, O Lord, our actions by thy holy inspirations, and carry them on by thy gracious assistance; that every prayer and work of ours may always begin from thee, and by thee be happily ended.

O Almighty and eternal God, who hast dominion over the living and the dead, and art merciful to all whom thou foreknowest shall be thine by faith and good works; we humbly beseech thee, that they for whom we have purposed to offer our prayers, whether this present world still detains them in the flesh, or the next world hath already received them divested of their bodies, may, by the clemency of thine own goodness and the intercession of thy saints, obtain pardon and full remission of all their sins; through our Lord Jesus Christ, who liveth and reigneth with thee, in the unity of the Holy Ghost, one God, world without end.

R. Amen.

V. May the Almighty and merciful Lord graciously hear us.

R. Amen.

V. May the souls of the faithful departed, through the mercy of God, rest in peace.

R. Amen.

An Act of Adoration to the Sacred Heart of Jesus

Adorable heart of Jesus, hypostatically united to the Eternal Word, and ever present in the holy Eucharist, receive my homage and the tribute of adoration which I here bring prostrate at the throne of thy glory. Mayest thou ever be reverenced and adored by all creatures; may the raising of hands, bending of knees, prostrations of the body practiced in our devotions; may the prayers, vows, and sacrifices of thy servants be ever agreeable and acceptable to thee. May the angels in heaven ever adore thee; and may the hearts of all thy faithful, especially that of the most blessed Virgin, ever breathe out in thy honor a most sweet odor and perfume of love, esteem, and respect. Sweet Jesus! receive this act of adoration; may it be acceptable in thy sight from my hands, and those of thy servants of this association, whom I particularly recom-mend to thee. Amen.

An Act of Consecration to the Sacred Heart of Jesus

To thee, O sacred heart of Jesus! to thee I devote and offer up my life, thoughts, words, actions, pains, and sufferings; the least part of my being shall no longer be employed, save only in loving, serving, honoring, and glorifying thee. Wherefore, O most sacred heart! be thou the sole object of my love, the protector of my life, the pledge of my salvation, and my secure refuge at the hour of my death. Be thou, 0 most bountiful heart, my justification at the throne of God, and screen me from his anger, which I have so justly merited. In thee I place all my confidence; and convinced as I am of my own weakness, I rely entirely on thy bounty. Annihilate in me all that is displeasing and offensive to thy divine Majesty; imprint thyself like a divine seal on my heart, that I may ever remember my obligations, and never be separated from thee. May my name, also, I beseech thee by thy tender bounty, ever be fixed and engraved in thee, O Book of Life; and may I ever be a victim consecrated to thy glory, ever burning with the flames of thy pure love, and entirely penetrated with it for all eternity; in this I place all my happiness; this is all my desire, to live and die in no other quality than that of thy devoted servant. Amen.

Through thy sacred heart, O Jesus! overflowing with all sweetness, we recommend to thee ourselves and all our concerns, our superiors, parents, relations, benefactors, friends, and enemies; take under thy protection this house, city, and kingdom; comfort all that are in affliction, and those who labor in the agony and pangs of death; look with compassionate mercy on the obstinate sinner, and on the poor suffering souls in purgatory. Be graciously pleased to bless those who are engaged and united with us in the holy confederacy of honoring and worshipping thee. Bless all, o bountiful Jesus! according to the extent of thy infinite goodness, mercy, and charity. Amen.

The Thirty Days Prayer to the Blessed Virgin Mary
In honor of the Sacred Passion of our Lord Jesus Christ

By the devout recital of this prayer, for the above space of time, we may mercifully hope to obtain our lawful request. It is particularly recommended as a proper devotion for every day in Lent, and all the Fridays throughout the year.

Even glorious and blessed Mary, Queen of Virgins, Mother of Mercy, hope and comfort of dejected and desolate souls, through that sword of sorrow which pierced thy tender heart whilst thy only Son, Jesus Christ our Lord, suffered death and ignominy on the Cross-through that filial tenderness and pure love he had for thee, grieving in thy grief, whilst from his cross be recommended thee to the care and protection of his beloved disciple St. John, take pity, I beseech thee, on my poverty and necessities; have compassion on my anxieties and cares; assist and comfort me in all my infirmities and miseries of what kind so ever.

Thou art the Mother of Mercies, the sweet consolatrix and refuge of the needy and the orphan, of the desolate and the afflicted. Cast, therefore, an eye of pity on a miserable forlorn child of Eve, and hear my prayer; for since in just punishment of my sins, I find myself encompassed by a multitude of evils, and oppressed with much anguish of spirit, whither can I fly for more secure shelter, o amiable Mother of my Lord and Savior Jesus Christ, than under the wings of thy maternal protection? Attend, therefore, I beseech thee, with an ear of pity and compassion to my humble and earnest request.

I ask it through the bowels of mercy of thy dear Son; through that love and condescension wherewith be embraced our nature, when, in compliance with the divine will, thou gavest thy consent, and whom, after the expiration of nine months, thou didst bring forth from the chaste enclosure of thy womb, to visit this world and bless it with his presence.

I ask it through that anguish of mind wherewith thy beloved Son, my dear Savior, was overwhelmed on Mount Olivet, when he besought his eternal Father to remove from him, if possible, the bitter chalice of his future passion.

I ask it through the three-fold repetition of his prayers in the Garden, from whence afterwards, with dolorous steps and mournful tears, thou didst accompany him to the doleful theatre of his death and sufferings.

I ask it through the welts and sores of his virginal flesh, occasioned by the cords and whips wherewith he was bound and scourged, when stripped of his seamless garment, for which his executioners afterwards cast lots.

I ask it through the seeds and ignominies by which he was insulted; the false accusations and unjust sentence by which he was condemned to death, and which he bore with heavenly patience.

I ask it through his bitter tears and bloody sweat, his silence and resignation, his sadness and grief of heart. I ask it through the blood which trickled from his royal and sacred head when struck with the sceptre of a reed, and pierced with his crown of thorns. I ask it through the excruciating torments he suffered, when his hands and feet' were fastened with gross nails to the tree of the cross.

I ask it through his vehement thirst, and bitter potion of vinegar and gall. I ask it through his dereliction on the cross, when he exclaimed, "My God! my God! why hast thou forsaken me?" I ask it through his mercy extended to the good thief, and through his recommending his precious soul and spirit into the hands of his eternal Father before he expired, saying, "All is consummated".

I ask it through the blood mixed with water which issued from his sacred side when pierced with a lance, and whence a flood of grace and mercy has flowed to us.

I ask it through his immaculate life, bitter passion, and ignominious death on the cross, at which nature itself was thrown into convulsions, by the bursting of rocks, rending the veil of the Temple, the earthquake, and darkness of the sun and moon.

I ask it through his descent into hell, where he comforted the' Saints of the old Law with his presence, and led captivity captive.

I ask it through his glorious victory over death, when he arose again to life on the third day, and through the joy which his appearance for forty days after gave thee his blessed Mother, his Apostles, and the rest of his Disciples; when in thine and their presence he miraculously ascended into heaven.

I ask it through the grace of the Holy Ghost, infused into the hearts of his Disciples when he descended upon them in the form of fiery tongues, and by which they were inspired with zeal in the conversion of the world, when they went to preach the Gospel.

I ask it through the awful appearance of thy Son at the last dreadful day, when he shall come to judge the living and the dead, and the world by fire.

I ask it through the compassion he bore thee in this life, and the ineffable joy thou didst feel at thine assumption into heaven, where thou art eternally absorbed in the sweet contemplation of his divine perfections. O glorious and ever blessed Virgin! comfort the heart of thy supplicant, by obtaining for me—

[Here mention or reflect on your lawful request, under the reservation of its being agreeable to the will of God, who sees whether it will contribute towards your spiritual good]

And as I am persuaded my divine Savior doth honor thee as his beloved Mother, to whom he refuses nothing, so let me speedily experience the efficacy of thy powerful intercession, according to the tenderness of thy maternal affection, and his filial loving heart, who mercifully granteth the requests and complieth with the desires of those that love and fear him.

Wherefore, O most blessed Virgin, beside the object of my present petition, and whatever else I may stand in need of, obtain for me also of thy dear Son, our Lord and our God, a lively faith, firm hope, perfect charity, true contrition of heart, unfeigned tears of compunction, sincere confession, condign satisfaction, abstinence from sin, love of God and my neighbor, contempt of the world, patience to suffer affronts and ignominies—nay, even, if necessary, an opprobrious death itself, for love of thy Son our Savior Jesus Christ.

Obtain likewise for me, O sacred Mother of God! perseverance in good works, performance of good resolutions, mortification of self-will, a pious conversation through life, and, at my last moments, strong and sincere repentance, accompanied by such a lively and attentive presence of mind as may enable me to receive the last Sacrament of the Church worthily and die in thy friendship and favor. Lastly, obtain through thy Son, I beseech thee, for the souls of my parents, brethren, relative and benefactors, both living and dead, life everlasting. Amen.

The Thirty Days Prayer

Glory, honor, and praise be to our Lord Jesus Christ. May all the world adore thee; blessed be thy holy name, who for us sinners vouchsafed to be born of an humble Virgin: and blessed be thine infinite goodness, who died upon the cross for our redemption.

O Jesus, Son of God, and Savior of mankind, we beseech thee to have mercy on us, and so dispose our lives here by thy grace, that we may hereafter rejoice with thee forever in thy heavenly kingdom. Amen.

Thirty Days Prayer to Our Blessed Redeemer in Honor of His Bitter Passion

O dear Jesus, my blessed Savior and Redeemer, the sweet comforter of all sad, desolate, and distressed souls; behold thy poor servant, humbly prostrate at the foot of thy holy cross, bewailing his misery, imploring thy mercy, and beseeching thee to take pity and compassion upon him in this his present and pressing affliction *(infirmity, poverty, temptation, trouble, or whatever other spiritual or corporeal necessity).* Hear my prayers, O assured refuge of all afflicted wretches! behold my tears, consider my sorrows, and remedy my distresses; for, finding myself encompassed with very grievous calamities, by reason of my great crimes, I know not whither to fly for succor, or to whom I may make my moan, but to thee, my meek and merciful Savior, with a full hope and confidence that thou, O my loving Redeemer, wilt vouchsafe to lend the ears of thy ordinary pity and accustomed clemency to the humble petition of thy poor child: and by that sweetness which thy blessed soul perceived at the time of thy alliance with our human nature, when resolving with the Father and the Holy Ghost to unite thy divine person to mortal flesh for man's salvation, thou didst send thy angel to thy Holy Virgin Mary with those happy tidings, and clothing thyself with our human nature, remained true God and true man for the space of nine months in her sacred womb.

By the anguish thou endured when, the time of thy designed passion drawing nigh, thou prayed to thy eternal Father, that if it might stand with his most divine providence, thou desired that that bitter chalice might pass away from thee! yet concluding with a most perfect act of resignation: Not my will, O heavenly Father, but thine be done.

By the outrageous injuries, shameful disgraces, cruel blows, contumelious blasphemies forged witnesses, false accusations, and unjust judgments, which thou, innocent Lamb! patiently endured; by the shackles which fettered thy limbs, the tears which flowed from thine eyes, the blood which trickled from thy whole body; by the fears, sorrows, and sadness of thy heart ; by the shame thou received in being stripped of thy garments, to hang naked on the cross, in the sight of thy sorrowful Mother, and in the presence of all the people.

By thy royal head crowned with thorns, and smitten with a reed; by thy thirst quenched with vinegar and gall; by thy side opened with a spear, whence issued blood and water, to refresh our souls with that living fountain of thy love and mercy; by the sharp nails wherewith thy tender hands and feet were cruelly pierced and fastened to the cross; by the recommendation of thy departing soul to thy heavenly Father, saying, Into thy hands I commend my spirit; by thy praying for thy enemies, saying, O Father, forgive them, for they know not what they do; by thy giving up the ghost, when thou cried out with a loud voice, My God, my God, why hast thou forsaken me? and then, bowing down thy most blessed head to impart the kiss of peace, said, It is consummated.

By the great mercy thou showed towards the penitent thief, saying, this day thou shalt be with me in Paradise; by thy descent into Limbus, and the joy thou communicated to the just souls therein detained ; by the glory of thy triumphant resurrection, and the consoling apparition thou frequently didst make for forty days' space to thy sacred Virgin Mother, to thy Apostles, and thy other chosen friends and servants; by thy admirable ascension, when, in the sight of thy Mother and thy Apostles, thou wast elevated into heaven; by the miraculous coming down of the Holy Ghost in the form of fiery tongues, whereby thou replenished the hearts of thy Disciples with thy love, and gave them strength and courage to plant thy faith in the whole world; by the dreadful day of general judgment, on which thou art to pass sentence on all mankind. By all those sorrows, joys, passions, compassions, and what soever else is near and dear to thee in heaven and on earth, take pity on me, O compassionate Redeemer, hear my prayers, and grant me that for which I now most humbly and heartily petition thee.

[Mention here what you desire, or reflect mentally upon it.]

Give me, o gracious Savior, speedy and efficacious feelings of thy divine succor and comfort, who, according to the accustomed sweetness of thy tender heart, art wont to grant the requests of them who really fear and love thee, even to their own soul's desire and satisfaction: bestow on me also, o my blessed Lord Jesus, a constant faith, a confident hope, a perfect charity, a cordial contrition, a sincere confession, a competent satisfaction, a diligent custody of myself from future failings, a heroic contempt of the world, a complete conquest of my passions, a zealous imitation of thy exemplary life and conversation, an entire accomplishment of my vows, an absolute mortification of my self-will, a willing readiness to die for thy love and honor, a final perseverance in grace and good works, a happy departure of my soul out of this world, with my perfect senses about me, thy holy sacraments to strengthen me; thyself, O dear Jesus, to comfort me; thy sacred Virgin Mother, with the saints, my particular patrons, to pray for me; and my good angel to conduct me to eternal rest, eternal life, and eternal happiness. Amen.

Printed in Great Britain
by Amazon